Pacesetting for Justice, Peace & Politics

Pacesetting

for Justice,

Peace &

Politics:

A Devotional

for Today's World

Philemon Nfor

ISBN: 979-8-9923580-0-1

KLG Press

This book is dedicated

to the memory of

Hon. Dr. Awudu Cyprian Mbaya

A TRIBUTE TO A HERO:
HON. DR. AWUDU CYPRIAN MBAYA!

Life is a gift, counted in years.
Years are a time frame, counted in events.
Events are opportunities, guided by vision;
Vision is a journey, carved out by care;
Care is a heart, playing out godly contents.

The heart is a container, clean or clouded;
The clean heart builds, not breaks hearts;
The clouded heart confuses, and robs hearts;
The cultivated heart clings, and cheers hearts;
The blessed heart is tons of blessings to hearts.

The heart of Hon. Awudu, was cleansed by the Divine;
The heart of Pa. Awudu, was crowded with love;
The heart of Dr. Awudu, was clinging and cheering humanity,
The heart, life, and vision of Hon. Dr. Awudu
gave many people meaning.

Oh, Pa Awudu, he had a gift of life from above;
Oh, Pa Awudu, your events meant life to many;
Oh, Pa Awudu, you transformed beyond imagination;
Oh, Pa Awudu,
Heaven must have told you when you got there;
Seventy-one years was great but you made it more so.

Daddy, Honorable, Doctor,
Servant of God,
The people's "Prince,"
The astute politician who knew when to exit,
Fare thee well!

We'll miss you, but your heart remains with us
and your marks will remind us,
Not just of you, but of the Lord you served,
And of the need for us to follow your footsteps,
Adieu, Papa! See you soon!

Foreword

Editing the Pacesetting books has been a journey encompassing over a quarter of a century. At the beginning of the 21st century, I was a seminary student while Rev. Nfor was obtaining his doctorate in theology at North American Baptist Seminary, Sioux Falls, SD. Through the years, Rev. Nfor and I have both raised families, touched the lives of many in pastoral ministry and been challenged concerning peace, justice and politics in each of our worlds. We have become life-long and steadfast friends, encountering the ups and downs of life on two very different continents.

During Philemon's (Rev. Nfor's) most recent trip to the United States I asked him once again why his daily Pacesetter devotions had not been compiled into a book. His answer was simple, "Many people have asked me the same thing, but I don't have enough time to undertake the project." So, I naively offered to edit and compile his extensive Pacesetter devotions into books. What a journey this has become!

While editing the first *Pacesetting in Christ-Like Living*, Philemon (Rev. Nfor) many times asked me "When are we going to be able to work on a political Pacesetting book?" My husband and I were invited to Yaoundé, Cameroon for the author's birthday celebration in March 2025. I felt a Pacesetting book on politics would be the perfect surprise for the big day, and *Peace, Justice and Politics* was born. Since Rev. Nfor did not have an opportunity to proof it before its final printing, I ask for grace for anything I have inadvertently misrepresented.

Reading these Pacesetting devotions has been like sitting by Rev. Nfor's side and listening to him speak about the world around him. May your experience be this rich as he points you toward God. My prayer is that I, and all of us, will be blessed to be a blessing in our world.

May you be blessed on your life's journey!

Karen Garrison

Acknowledgements

I count it a blessing to be able to bring Rev. Nfor's Pacesetter to life in book form. While he has many to thank, here are a few who helped with that process.

Thank you to both of our families who have helped bring the book to life.

- Len, my husband for encouraging me during the many hours I poured into editing the manuscript.
- Heather and Joe, for the hours leading me through the editing process. Sarah, for helping with the book cover design. I really appreciate her artistic flare.
- The Nfor family with great gratitude for their assistance as I edited this book.
- Our Patmos family, and your care for Daddy Rev. Nfor. You are loved.

May God bless you all.

Karen Garrison

Table of Contents

FOR HOW LONG, LORD!

I was born into a village with two Fons. This context taught me at a very young age that leadership can be a problem. I have no clue of the cause but know what it means to have two rulers on one throne or two thrones in one leadership rule! Before I got to my teenage years I saw villages in conflict. The conflict's cause, effects and solutions are as simple as ABC, but it has taken lives, property, joy, happiness and good neighborliness away because of nothing but the show of physical and financial power. But for how long?

In my teenage years I learned of a president who had taken my country to independence. By the time I got into advanced history class I started learning what devastation leadership can cause when it manipulates, steals, cheats, and fails to punish those who do wrong, but rather promotes them. I learned what happens when leadership fails to reward those who do right and abandons them to their self-survival struggles. When that president left power, the celebration was great. I remember the National Radio Station reading names of many people who had succumbed to the state's killing machine! Shortly after, we shouted, marched, put stickers of "My President" on our school bags and looked forward to a democratic one-party state. Hahaha!

Guns could not stop the expansion to multi-party politics, and we celebrated again, certain that now strong democratic debates would transform parliament. Politics taught us that strong institutions make for a strong nation and a strong world. Really? Political theorists forgot and still have not realized that institutions are made by men, and their running depends on the state of their hearts. Yes, God helped, and the parliament became strong and vibrant. As if to fulfill scripture, **"It pleased the Lord for the sake of his righteousness to make his law great and glorious" (Isaiah 42:21, NIV).**

But: The hearts of those who lead are the same ones who have led from my teenage years through today. They are the same people whose names I learned as leaders in my elementary school lessons. I know them still after over half a century. They are the same who have no retirement age limits and do not seem to have had their hearts changed. They made and make institutions and tailor them to their personal gains.

And the people?

"But this is a people plundered and looted, all of them trapped in pits or hidden away in prisons. They have become plunder, with no one to rescue them; they have been made loot, with no one to say, "Send them back" (Isaiah 42:22, NIV).

The people have struggled! We have suffered! But leadership has watched, laughed, drunk their wine in celebration of their swollen bank accounts, built strong physical walls around their houses and hired security guards to accompany them even to the toilet. The people were numb for a while, unable to react.

Then: **"So he [God] poured out on them [the leaders] his burning anger, the violence of war. It enveloped them in**

14

flames, yet they did not understand; it consumed them, but they did not take it to heart" (Isaiah 42:25, NIV). How can the leaders take the pain of war to heart when their hearts are numb, the laws protect them while sending the innocent to jail, wars kill children of the innocent, and the populace suffers while they live in sheltered cities. The battered education system is further preventing the possibility of the oppressed from ever getting to power. Meanwhile leaders' children are preparing in schools abroad to come and continue from where the parents will leave?

God! How long will it take You to remove these hearts of stone and implant hearts of flesh for freedom in my village, freedom in my region(s), freedom in my country, and freedom in a world where even the supposedly strongest institution, the United Nations, defends the interest of the strong and batters the battered? For how long will You wait to change hearts to let leaders love people and serve them as they should? For how long Lord? For how long? *Have mercy Lord and save us*, in Jesus' Name.

SEE - YOUR KING ON THE THRONE FOR YOU!

What is giving you fear? I like the fact that your God goes with and before you to ensure that all is well. I heard a story of someone whose documents for promotion got lost in their office. For many years, he looked for them and did not find them. He came to a service and complained to the minister preaching that day and they prayed for the documents to be found. A few days later, the man with the lost documents was sent on mission, a cleaner came to clean the office, saw an envelope under the carpet, opened and presented it to the boss. Behold, it was the missing documents. Men can rule kingdoms but God rules over them all.

King David declared: **"The Lord has established his throne in heaven, and his kingdom rules over all" (Psalm 103:19, NIV).** That God has established His throne in heaven is an indication of His sovereignty. He has both power and authority above and beyond all. His Kingdom which rules over all indicates that there are "kingdoms" in which people, powers, and principalities rule. Unfortunately, we live in a world where every little responsibility over an entity is turned into a kingdom in which the "servant" becomes an autocratic king who seeks to molest and frustrate those they are supposed to help accomplish tasks. Those kingdoms do not bring peace or joy. Thank God He rules over them.

Beloved in the Lord, as you step out to face the kingdoms over you at work, in your political party, even in your community, or family, bear in mind that:

- Because your King rules over all, you do not have to be afraid of whatever comes your way. Let fear not rule over your heart, even in the presence of the great and wicked who stand before you. Your God is greater!

- Call on your King who rules over all and let Him know that you need His attention. Often, it is not the power of the opposing kingdom that brings pain and keeps us under bondage, but our failure to hand the troubling situation to the King who rules over all. When you hand it to Him, wait patiently. Do not forget, **"No one who hopes in you [God] will ever be put to shame" (Psalm 25:3a, NIV).**

Go out with joy and faith, in prayer and hope; face your distractions with boldness but also in humility. Serve well, judiciously, and dedicatedly. Your God will not let you be put to shame, as He will bring victory to you, in Jesus' Name, Amen.

HONOR THE ALL WISE AND WISDOM-GIVING GOD

For more than two decades of their marriage, my good friend and relative fought with his wife both verbally and physically on almost a daily basis. When they gave their lives to Christ, the change was drastic. I remember her calling me to tell me, "Reverend, my husband went to the village and has called me to tell me that he loves me." It was like their marriage had started again from scratch. God gave each of them a new mindset that enabled them to see things so differently and lovingly. He is an all-wise God!

The world spends fabulous amounts of money searching for peace all over the world. People spend much money and time developing abilities to become facilitators and mediators of peace initiatives. Unfortunately, the same world and the same people are antagonistic to Christianity, not realizing that all peacebuilding, conflict management, and peacekeeping efforts are second-best strategies, consuming much money. The best solution for peace in individuals, between individuals, and between communities is a genuine commitment to the life and principles of Christ. Jesus is the Prince of Peace and the Mediator between God and mankind. He gave His life for it and lives for it *now*.

An honest surrender to Jesus is a great source of wisdom and peace. However, sometimes we find Christians fighting or doing other things that hamper peace. Why? For three major reasons:

First, many people call themselves Christians when they are just churchgoers. They have not tasted the fruit they hold in their hands. So, they talk about Christianity but do not live it. Christianity is a relationship. It must be lived to have an impact.

Second, Christianity is a growth process. The younger the Christian is in faith, not age, the more the probability for him or her to make errors that could jeopardize peace.

Third, when we are faced with complicated problems, it is hard to know what to do to solve them. Failing to ask God for wisdom may mean the use of wisdom not led by the Spirit. The result? Fighting!

Young Christians, old Christians and, in fact, even non-Christians have access to Divine wisdom for peace and all other needs for relationships within the human race. **"For the Lord gives wisdom; from his mouth come knowledge and understanding....Then you will understand what is right and just and fair - every good path. For wisdom will enter your heart, and knowledge will be pleasant to your soul" (Proverbs 2:6, 9-10, NIV).** There is no greater source of wisdom than God.

Beloved in the Lord, are you in a situation that looks very complex, and peace is even threatened? Are you not sure of how to handle it? Whether it is a personal or professional issue you need to handle, ask God for wisdom. He will direct you in handling it. Ask God in prayer. He will answer and wisdom will enter your heart. If God has given you peace in your heart and is helping you live wisely in your daily living, honor Him. Celebrate Him and with the blessing of peace you possess, bless others. This week and beyond, celebrate the God of all wisdom and you will be blessed, in Jesus' Name.

GRACE OVERFLOWS UNTO MERCY!

If one considers the political and economic weight of Germany, one can be tempted to ask if God really hates sin. Germany was largely responsible for the start of World War I. The holocaust tells the story of the wickedness of German leaders who wanted to wipe the Jews from the surface of the earth. The partitioning of Africa into the colonial property for various European nations was done in Berlin, Germany. Why did God not destroy that nation and even wipe it from the map, even for the sake of the Jews, His chosen people? God is more interested in saving than in sinking, in rescuing than in scattering, and in building than in destroying. It is more important for God to keep His own than to kill their enemies. Even for the enemies of God's people as well as for the disobedience of His children, grace abounds and overflows to mercy. **"But where sin increased, grace increased all the more," (Romans 5:20b, NIV).**

When I see the evil going on in the world; when I see democracy hanging by a thread and producing more despots than democrats in Africa; when I see the multitudes of unemployed and underemployed youths around me and tired statesmen deceiving themselves that they are not old and refusing to leave space for the young; when I see the educated manipulating the skills of the uneducated for selfish gains at even local levels; my heart is filled with pain, and my eyes with tears. But then, I remember that favor overflows to mercy.

Beloved child of God, if you are at the receiving end of pain and evil, wickedness and witchcraft; even if you are self-judged and pitifully self-condemned, wipe your tears! God's grace is greater than your error of former willful wrongdoing, and His power is mightier than your greatest antagonist. His grace will favor you and His mercy will visit your situation.

For you, your family, village, region or nation, make this confession; pray this prayer:

"Do not withhold your mercy from me, Lord; may your love and faithfulness always protect me. For troubles without number surround me; my sins have overtaken me, and I cannot see. They are more than the hairs of my head, and my heart fails within me. Be pleased to save me, Lord; come quickly, Lord, to help me" (Psalm 40:11-13, NIV).

In His infinite grace and mercy, God shall answer, and it will be well with you and yours, in Jesus' Name.

WORSHIP YOUR REIGNING KING!

Ah, the Lord reigns. England has had about sixty-two kings in their history, and since the union of Scotland and England in 1707, they have had 13 kings. My village has had eleven or twelve chiefs (kings) in her own history. I concentrate on kings (or queens) and chiefs (now called fons) because their thrones are hereditary. Only death takes one away. But the universe has had one King since He created it, made humanity live in it, and has directed its affairs ever since. This great King has the final say in the "who's who" of the world. **"He changes times and seasons; he deposes kings and raises up others. He gives wisdom to the wise and knowledge to the discerning" (Daniel 2:21, NIV).** He is the King of Kings.

The traditional, political and economic power of kings and rulers of this world may look very strong and invincible. Some even threaten the life and safety of others. War in the English-speaking part of Cameroon has reduced the aura of our much-dreaded fons. Some have been killed mercilessly and one held by young men in the bush for a long while now. That could never be imagined before. Individual rulers like Vladimir Putin exercise much authority and power, oppress, kill, and extend or try to extend their territorial rule by force. They forget that others have been on that route before, and the King of Kings, is **"The Lord [who] brings death and makes alive; he brings down to the grave and raises up" (1 Samuel 2:6, NIV).** The history of Europe has a whole period dedicated to despots; those who ruled like they had the final say. That time is over. Africa has despotic monarchs who disguise themselves as elected presidents, always emerging as the people's leaders from well-staged elections with well-crafted results. They are unpopular "people's leaders!"

Beloved in the Lord, honor the king and respect his orders in the Lordship of Christ, but worship the Lord. He is King over all, and soon you will join the heavenly beings in the song of ultimate and final victory.

"The seventh angel sounded his trumpet, and there were loud voices in heaven, which said: 'The kingdom of the world has become the kingdom of our Lord and of his Messiah, and he will reign for ever and ever.' And the twenty-four elders, who were seated on their thrones before God, fell on their faces and worshiped God, saying: 'We give thanks to you, Lord God Almighty, the One who is and who was, because you have taken your great power and have begun to reign'" (Revelation 11:15-17, NIV).

Do not wait for the end times to worship this great King. Worship Him now and always. He will be exalted and will lift people to Himself and bless you, in Jesus' Name.

LOVE YOUR NEIGHBOR!

Have you ever thought that loving your neighbor could be a protection for you? A sister told me that one day she was sleeping deeply with the children in the house. Without their noticing it, an enemy stole his way into the house through the kitchen door, opened the gas and went out locking the door behind him. The front door was also locked. Before the smell of the gas could wake them up, the house was filled with gas, and they were suffocating under it. It took a neighbor who noticed that there was a problem, rushed to the house, realized what was happening and broke the kitchen door from outside, so they could be freed. The neighbor saved them. What if they had had a bad relationship with that neighbor?

The Gibeonites lied in an attempt to make Israel good neighbors. **"... when the people of Gibeon heard what Joshua had done to Jericho and Ai, they resorted to a ruse: They went as a delegation whose donkeys were loaded with worn-out sacks and old wineskins, cracked and mended. Then they went to Joshua in the camp at Gilgal and said to him and the Israelites, 'We have come from a distant country; make a treaty with us"** (Joshua 9:3-4, 6, NIV).

They were acting out of fear. They succeeded. **"Then Joshua made a treaty of peace with them to let them live, and the leaders of the assembly ratified it by oath"** (Joshua 9:15, NIV). They lived with Israel safely and in peace.

When our first night watchman did not do his job good enough, a good neighbor to our church made it a personal responsibility to keep the church safe. Good neighborliness is important.

Child of God, for your own safety, know your neighbors and love them. I come to you with a plea for a prayer of love for a great neighbor. With a population of over two hundred thirty million, Nigeria is not a nation to be ignored by Africa or the rest of the world. Nigeria exports the best and the worst. It has the economic power to influence Africa and the global economy. Nigeria has the military and intellectual might to contribute to stability in the sub-region. Good, godly leadership in Nigeria could have a global impact, and would certainly have great positive ripple effects on the African continent. Please, wherever you are in the world, remember that in the global village that the world has turned into, the neighbor is not just the person next door but the person in need. Their need is your need; their pain is your pain, and their gain is your gain. May God bring forth good leadership, good governance to Nigeria and through that, bless our world, in Jesus' Name.

FOR ANY COURSE, THINK "ME" BEFORE "US!"

The first time I experienced a public revolt was in my second year in secondary school, when as a class we decided that we would not accept the history teacher to teach us. We heard from Form 2A to Form 2D that she spent time talking about herself rather than teaching. For this reason, we planned as a class and kept her out of our classroom. It was so serious that the administration abandoned our class, but our class master, a physics teacher, taught us history. It turned out to be a great decision for us as that history teacher played around and taught nothing. Bringing change in the family, in your place of work or in the society as a whole; be it a village, city or nation may take a crowd but often, it must have an individual who stands out to lead with all the prospects, cost and risk involved. If you desire change in anything, think and talk about "What I will do" before you talk of "What we should do."

In the gathering on Martin Luther King Jr.'s Day, the American president, Joe Biden gave a significant reminder while talking about the hero who was being celebrated in these words: "He followed the path of Moses, a leader of inspiration, calling on the people not to be afraid and to always, always, as my grandfather would say, keep the faith. He followed the path of Joseph; a believer in dreams, in the divinity they carry, in the promise they hold. And like John the Baptist, he prepared us for the greater hope ahead, one who came to bear witness to the Light. Reverend Dr. Martin Luther

King Jr. was a nonviolent warrior for justice, who followed the word and the way of his Lord and his Savior."[1]

Moses, Joseph, David, Nehemiah, John the Baptist, Jesus and Paul are a few Biblical figures who stand out in their roles in liberating God's people in their times. Nelson Mandela, Martin Luther, Martin Luther King Jr., Mahatma Gandi, and a host of African nationalists in each country, are people who denied themselves pleasure, leisure, comfort, safety, and even life for a positive social change. Because they stood out, they had followers and accomplished great courses in their lifetimes or paved the way for the accomplishments after them. Individual contribution is critical to the success of collective action. Consider, "Me" before you talk about "Us!" Jesus was appointing Peter, who had cut off the ear of someone who wanted to arrest Jesus, and who had already proven his personal engagement for the Lord and the disciples. Peter looked and saw that Apostle John was following them. **"When Peter saw him, he asked, 'Lord, what about him?' Jesus answered, 'If I want him to remain alive until I return, what is that to you? You must follow me'"** (John 21:21-22, NIV). Peter obeyed!

If you have a passion for your church to reach out and grow, put your heart in prayer and personal engagement in it; then, call others to follow you. If you have the passion for change in your society: village, city or nation, ask God to show you what to do and no

---

[1] Joe Biden, *Remarks by President Biden Honoring Dr. Martin Luther King, Jr.* January 16, 2023, Ebenezer Baptist Church, Atlanta, Georgia, whitehouse.gov

matter how little it is, do it. It is easier to reach people's hearts with a message of a little action than to reach them with the eloquence and wordiness of inactivity. Sometimes you must get involved before God catapults you to the top. As God leads, take the first step and call on others to follow. Be the Martin Luther King Jr. of your time in your own situation, and the Lord will bless you and bless many through you, in Jesus' Name.

LET THE KING OF KINGS LEAD!

In my few years of living I have had the opportunity of experiencing the rule of two village leaders in each of the two villages where I grew up, and two presidents in my nation. These regimes have something in common but have not been the same. In all of them, the changes have been significant, one great and the others, not so good. The point is, change in leadership means change in policies, approaches, alliances, vision and consequently, change in life's experiences in the village, nation or wherever the leader exercises authority. That is the difference between human and divine leadership.

Change in human leadership brings changes because people think, view and approach things differently, even when they see them the same. They are influenced by their experiences, backgrounds, and the environment in which they live. The most important influence is their selfishness or selflessness. Who they lead for is essential to what they do and the results they get.

Beloved in the Lord, the King of Kings and the God of the Universe is worth following. His rulership has never changed and will never change. **"Jesus Christ is the same yesterday and today and forever" (Hebrews 13:8, NIV).** God's character, ways, purposes, will, direction, and plan for humanity have never changed and will never change. The divine *truth* as revealed in scripture has never changed and will never change. God is not a permissive leader who changes His ways in line with what people think or say. No! His will and ways are perfect, and He is absolutely faithful to them.

Dear friend, no matter how intelligent, philosophical or scientific humanity becomes, God remains the King of all, and His supremacy cannot be challenged. He is not a creation of human wisdom; He is the Creator of all humanity. Because of the perfection of His will and ways, nothing He says needs correction and nothing He says is changeable. **"God is not human, that he should lie, not a human being, that he should change his mind. Does he speak and then not act? Does he promise and not fulfill?" (Numbers 23:19, NIV)**. Therefore, dear friend, in all you do, think or say; in every aspect of your life, let God, the King of kings lead you. He is selflessly loving and will get you to your best in life. Follow Him in all things and it will be well with you, in Jesus' Name.

PRAY FOR YOUR KING!

Leaders are a group of people who, most probably, receive the greatest criticism, the harshest response and the least encouragement from those they lead. Consider the case of British Prime Minister Liz Truss! It can be joyous to be the longest reigning leader wherever his or her leadership is exercised, but it cannot be that easy to be the shortest-lasting leader in the history of a nation. The seven weeks at 10 Downing Street (the official residence of the prime minister) must have been her most difficult time in life. She may never have such a tough time again. Since she handed over power, we hear nothing of her. She may be struggling with regrets and even depression, but life continues like nothing ever went wrong. Pray for your king and your leaders!

Saul, the first king of Israel, was the people's choice. The people asked for a king much to the displeasure of God. They went ahead and got their king using their own criteria. While God looked at the heart in choosing leaders, Israel looked at the physical and the external. **"Kish had a son named Saul, as handsome a young man as could be found anywhere in Israel, and he was a head taller than anyone else" (1 Samuel 9:2, NIV).** They wanted him as their king and God sent Samuel to anoint Saul as king of Israel. But when duty called, he and Israel stood before Goliath helpless. For forty days, the Philistine giant made a fool of them until David arrived, got permission from Saul, went after Goliath and killed him. In bringing down Goliath, David, God's own choice as leader in Israel, brought down Saul's pride, confidence, popularity, joy and eventually his kingship. Just imagine Saul's morale when he heard Israel singing, to welcome him from the war in which Goliath was killed;

"When the men were returning home after David had killed the Philistine, the women came out from all the towns of Israel to meet King Saul with singing and dancing, with joyful songs and with timbrels and lyres. As they danced, they sang: 'Saul has slain his thousands, and David his tens of thousands'" (1 Sam. 18:6-7, NIV).

That was hard for Saul. As a result of this situation, **"Saul was afraid of David, because The Lord was with David but had departed from Saul" (1 Samuel 18:12, NIV).** When God's choice is with the opposition, the village, city or nation cannot be at peace.

Beloved, pray for your king and your leaders. Yes, all people in authority are placed there by God but:

- When the people do not seek God's guidance, their choice for leader could be one who would rather bring them pain not joy.

- God may choose a leader but what the people want from the leader is not at all in line with God's desire for the people. They can pressure him or her to do what is liked rather than what is right. When the wrong thing is liked, it eventually brings pain and destruction.

- When the people's choice is in charge and God's choice is in the opposition, a long-drawn battle destroys people before it eventually destroys the leader if he or she does not discern the times and give up.

- When the people do not pray for the king, he can take people hostage for his selfish agenda and create a kingdom for self and family in perpetuity. Prayers can lift up but they can also bring down for the uplifting of the right person.

Dearly beloved, pray, **"for kings and all those in authority, that we may live peaceful and quiet lives in all godliness and holiness" (1 Timothy 2:2, NIV)** and it will be well with you, in Jesus' Name.

GOD CAN USE THE YOUNG!

I grew to know that wisdom is found in the gray-haired elderly. Most of the time, those of us who were young either did not participate in any discussion, or only listened and made no comment at all. We were told that the time for the young is in the future when we would have learning and experience. The problem is, there is no definition for the age of experience, though the learning part may be visible from certificates. Do young people really not have much to offer?

I was almost caught in a trap when a village crowned a teenager as their fon. My immediate reaction was that the kingmakers might want to do something and decided to crown the young man to just cover up their acts. Then, I remembered that it is not so much about age but about what God can do with a person as His instrument.

Josiah was eight years old when he became the king of Israel. His reign marked one of the greatest in the history of that nation. How? He took Israel back to God. He became king at a time when Israel had drifted so far from God they did not even know where the Book of the Law was. The Temple was in ruins and the Book was buried there. During Josiah's reign, repair works were done on the temple and in the process, they found the Book of the Law.

When the king got the words of the Book, he tore his clothes in distress. Then he ordered,

"Go and inquire of the Lord for me and for the people and for all Judah about what is written in this book that has been found. Great is the Lord's anger that burns against us because those who have gone before us have not obeyed the words of this book; they have not acted in accordance with all that is written there concerning us" (2 Kings 22:13, NIV).

The people read the book, did a total cleansing of the Temple and the land and renewed their covenant with God.

Friends in the Lord, the restoration of our nation, and the nations of the world, to the peace, joy and development that has been so taken away, is a factor of our restoration to truth and justice. It is anchored on Divine revelation and empowered mostly by faith in Jesus as Savior and Lord. The wrongness around us is too big for reforms to fix, though we badly need reforms. Our calamities are too much for humanity to fix without Divine intervention.

Oh, may God help us to see that the elderly who are experienced in doing wrong can only lead people towards the direction of destruction.

Oh, that God would give us leaders after His own heart, even young leaders. May they be leaders who can listen; leaders who can lead us to a life that celebrates God, not power, not money, not positions, but God! Please join me to pray for such leaders, so that we can be blessed, in Jesus' Name.

BE A PEACEMAKER

Peace is not just the absence of war, but people living together in oneness of heart and purpose. Concern for each other and working for the good of each other is fundamental to social well-being.

One of my worst childhood memories is of our church being sealed, and us worshipping in someone's home. Without going into the conflict that saw people imprisoned by the church and others backsliding for the rest of their lives, I wonder why the people aspiring to lead the church unravel both peace and the institution itself through their fight for positions within it. In church, in our social groups and in the nation, seeking leadership often threatens peace. If leaders are peacemakers, the process of taking power and maintaining it should be characterized by peace.

If you are the head of the family, you are the leader, and your presence and activities should bring peace, unity and progress.

As you seek progress in your family, at your workplace, in your social group, in your church, in your municipality, and in your nation, remember the words of our Lord, **"Blessed are the peacemakers, for they will be called children of God" (Matthew 5:9, NIV).** He has not said, "Blessed are the developers."

- Development is good, but peace is more important and primary. A developed Ukraine was reduced to rubble in a matter of days, for lack of peace!

- With peace, development will come. Without peace, development is a bribe that eventually ends as rubble.
- When war and a build-up of weapons produce peace, it instills fear, suspicion, uncertainty, and eventually, another war. Peace is a product of essentially two things, justice and love.
- Peacemakers are children of God and children of God are peacemakers. They promote justice and love in their families, communities and nations.

"Blessed are the peacemakers...!" Beloved in the Lord, be a peacemaker:

- Pray for justice and love in your family, community and nation, so you can have peace.
- Be an element of reconciliation and not a winner. Greater peace comes when you create understanding and agreement between disagreeing individuals and groups than when you help one win.

Work to reconcile! That is the investment for peace that Christ will validate, and He will bless you as a peacemaker. Be a peacemaker and be blessed, in Jesus' Name.

HELLO POLITICS: I AM A CHRISTIAN!

I got up early on the morning of October 1, 2024, with a smile on my face after a good night's rest from a very tiring day. But the smile faded away very fast because the first thing I saw on my WhatsApp was the killing of friends I know very well. They are the father and mother of a colleague pastor. More seriously, this is the third killing in that same village by the same group of people within two months or so. Meetings have been held on the issue of the relationship between the two tribal peoples involved.

As I tried to stop any tears falling from my eyes, I got this quote from our group, "Politics is too serious a matter to be left to the politicians" (de Galle)[2] This seemed relevant because the killings took place within a particular political context in our nation that has been a thorn in the flesh of the nation for nearly a decade now. The political will to solve it has not been as forthcoming as is needed to get peace for the nation. One of my great mentors in the pastoral ministry was an astute politician whose commitment to Christ and the preaching of the gospel was unequivocal. He preached the gospel in his political life and exited the stage of politics and life with clean hands. He is only one, like a single star from among very few shining in the darkest night you can imagine. Why is it that some of the most wicked people the world has known have either

---

[2] Charles de Galle. The Socratic Method, inspiringquotes.us

been politicians or their activities have been connected to politics? Think of Adolf Hitler, Joseph Stalin, Napoleon Bonaparte, Mao Zedong, King Leopold II and his wicked rule in Congo, and Idi Amin Dada. Then think of Saddam Hussein and Osama Bin Ladin and his influence on life for political reasons. Americans stood at the crossroads between a rock and a hard place in a presidential election where most would have been happy to have both candidates out of the way. Perplexingly, one of them played a Christian to get the votes of the Christians with many falling for his absurd "Christian story." But there are Christian politicians, some of whom are in the senate and the house! Where are they? Where are Christians when all these wicked people take over to terrify their nations and the world around them?

Why does truth not seem to play any part in political discussion or political gaming? Is politics not simply the science of public management? How can something so serious and so important be left in the hands of professionals? No! Many politicians, especially in Africa, are not even professional politicians, but instead are using politics as an exploitive aspect of their lives. Many of them come with the mindset that if you cannot be crude and bad-hearted, you should not even try politics. Hello politics, I am a Christian! My Bible tells me that God is most concerned about the well-being and safety of His people. God is concerned about the just and equitable distribution of the resources with which He has endowed us as people of the world. He has given us leaders, in politics and elsewhere, to ensure that rightness is done. For those who can but fold their arms and watch, and for those who can do right but choose to be selfish and destructive, God is watching! God's reason for choosing leaders, including politicians is clear,

"For rulers hold no terror for those who do right, but for those who do wrong. Do you want to be free from fear of the one in authority? Then do what is right and you will be commended. For the one in authority is God's servant for your good. But if you do wrong, be afraid, for rulers do not bear the sword for no reason. They are God's servants, agents of wrath to bring punishment on the wrongdoer" (Romans 13:3-4, NIV).

There is an even clearer text on this matter:

"Submit yourselves for the Lord's sake to every human authority: whether to the emperor, as the supreme authority, or to governors, who are sent by him to punish those who do wrong and to commend those who do right. For it is God's will that by doing good you should silence the ignorant talk of foolish people. Live as free people, but do not use your freedom as a cover-up for evil; live as God's slaves" (1 Peter 2:13-16, NIV).

It is clear that the rule of political leaders is to ensure good governance, which simply means rewarding those who do right and punishing those who do wrong. They make the laws to guide people into rightness and implement them to ensure obedience, justice, and equity. When they fail to punish those who do wrong, evil prevails and reproduces in society, leading to a downward spiral of morality, chaos, disorder, and death. This text also reminds us that the God who chooses leaders guides their hearts. When this is not the case, the nation will only groan because it is righteousness that exalts a nation. Righteousness comes from Christ in the heart, transforming it and guiding it to right action and people-oriented policies. Without God, politics is a game of interest. With God, politics is a management tool for the good of the masses, including the politicians! Hello, Politics: I am a Christian and would like to tell you that God wants your heart and mind for your good and the good of the people under whose charge He has appointed you.

It has been a historical disfavor for Christians to sit back and criticize politics and politicians and simply look at them and ignore what they do. Sadly, they rule the nation. They make the laws. They ensure its application or lack of it. They execute managerial policies, even deciding whether the Christians themselves will be free or not. Beloved in the Lord, it is time you step out of your comfort zone and seek public office. When you get there and gain the freedom to do what is right or to do what you can, remember that God sent you there for the good of the nation, not for your bank account. If there will be a future for the world at large, it will be with the light of God shining through those who confess Him in the dark skies of politics for the glory of God and the sake of His people. Christian, wake up to political consideration and pray like you never have prayed before. Politician, wake up to the call of God and transform your political career or endeavors and it shall be well with you, in Jesus' Name.

WORSHIP THE FAITHFUL GOD!

Faithfulness means the willingness, ability and commitment to keep promises. Lack of faithfulness is the world's greatest reason for distrust, quarrels and wars.

- Quarrels and fights break out between couples when one distrusts the other's commitment to the relationship,
- Families break apart when promises are broken, and distrust comes in,
- Villages go to war when trust is abused and promises are broken,
- The world is at the brink of war because NATO, led by America broke the promise they had made (when Germany was united) never to expand to the East. It is strange, even pathetic to think that Putin wanted Russia to be admitted into NATO so they could fight world terrorism together. His idea was rejected. Broken promises, distrust, and a show of power on the side of Europe and America, and Russia's struggle to regain greatness and ensure her own safety, has produced a new Cold War that has opened a new arms race. It has made these so-called great powers spend much on sophisticated weapons in a world where millions die of hunger. Sadly, for the first time since the end of the Cold War and the Berlin Wall falling in Germany, there is fear of a possible World War, in a world with nuclear weapons where massive killings will be easy.

Faithlessness or breaking promises is dangerous!

Thank God for God! He is faithful. **"The Lord is righteous in all his ways and faithful in all he does" (Psalm 145:17, NIV).** His faithfulness is not for Himself because man does not contribute to the completeness of God. His faithfulness is for you, **"But the Lord is faithful, and he will strengthen you and protect you from the evil one" (2 Thessalonians 3:3, NIV).**

Therefore, may you join me and be faithful, as I join the Psalmist in this commitment: **"I will exalt you, my God the King; I will praise your name for ever and ever. Every day I will praise you and extol your name for ever and ever. Great is the Lord and most worthy of praise" (Psalm 145:1-3a, NIV).** He has promised. His faithfulness endures forever. May He bless and keep you, and give you peace, in Jesus' Name.

SEEK GOD'S JUSTICE FIRST!

When I have a little time to relax, I sometimes watch African movies. They are not the ones on high streets, or in bars and mansions but the traditional ones that depict the cultures of the land. Most of them center on African connectedness to the gods and the ancestors. Mostly, you have either a wicked ruler or a wicked man that wants the throne and fights for it with wicked schemes. In the end, such wickedness is judged by the "gods of our ancestors" and the wicked perish without mercy. I can identify with some of the realities in these narratives because I grew up in a traditional setting where there was no prison in the village, yet people judiciously paid their fines levied by the Traditional Council. But, when the throne was wicked, suffering lasted throughout the chief's lifetime.

Today, the multiplicity of both administrators including the village fon, city mayor, divisional officer and legal armed groups including the police, gendarmerie, council police, and vigilantes has not made it easier for wickedness to be dealt with. Instead, the wicked can be protected when they have the money or the influence to lobby and win the hearts of those in charge. In a system where justice is bought and sold to the highest bidder, justice ceases to have meaning and administration and law-keeping are nothing more than a means of making money. So, instead of running to the law courts in search of justice, people run to the king, the divisional officer, the mayor and others because they can speak authoritatively and command action. Of course, the wicked like to use money and get their way, but for the remainder of us God says: **"Many seek an audience with a ruler, but it is from the Lord that one gets justice" (Proverbs 29:26, NIV).**

Beloved, if you are oppressed and you have no access to the ruler, relax in the presence of God who has given you access to His throne through prayer. Talk to Him and trust Him. He will stand with you and ensure that you get justice. Yes, He may be taking time but long is not forever. Justice will come and you will be free.

If you have access to authority and the means to convince them to do your will against the weak and vulnerable, know the God of the Universe is the God of Justice. He sets up rulers to reward those who do right and punish those who do wrong. If rulers do otherwise, God will take over His rule in their hands. You will be as surprised as the wicked rulers or throne seekers in African movies, who are always taken by surprise when justice is being rendered to them. Life on earth is short. God's time will come, and His incorruptible justice shall reign forever. In all you seek and do, let the Ruler of all the earth judge you. When He frees your conscience now, He will free your body, bless you and you can be sure that your soul will enjoy eternal freedom when the time comes. Before then, you will be a channel of blessing to many people, in Jesus' Name.

SAFETY IS IN GOD ALONE!

What a world we live in! It is said that if you want peace, prepare for war. But who spends so much money on weapons and soldiers, builds sophisticated, state-of-the-art war machinery and is not eager to put it into use at the slightest provocation? Russia invaded a country to ensure security in her backyard and keep the USA *and* Europe from being able to attack her easily. Europe and the USA have had those same concerns and actions in the past. Must there be war for peace to reign? Is history not confirming the word of God that relationship building is better for peace, than preparing for war to have peace?

Both the European Union and the United Nations are products of brutal wars, after which the nations concerned agreed to work together to avoid wars happening again. Two major problems remain.

- The major powers with the rights of veto (meaning those whose one vote can stop a decision) have been working to protect their interest and are not in a close or good relationship with each other. They are in two blocks: China and Russia on one hand, and the USA, Britain, and France on the other. The fear remains that these two fronts can still start a World War because the rest of the world *mostly* supports one side or the other.

- No trust has been built over the years despite all the negotiations they have been having. Investments in the military for these nations and in the world at large are growing because of the fear of attack! How much truer can the Bible be when it says, **"Fear of man will prove to be a snare, but whoever trusts in the Lord is kept safe" (Proverbs 29:25, NIV).**

- Fear of man is something that enslaves, entangles, and does not promote peace. The solution to fearing man is trusting in God. That means:

- Trust God enough to live by His guidance. His most important guidance to prevent quarrels and wars is to have good relationships. In His death, Christ unites, **"For he himself is our peace, who has made the two groups one and has destroyed the barrier, the dividing wall of hostility" (Ephesians 2:14, NIV).** If only the world could let the love of Christ drop the barriers of race and superpowers versus beggar powers, north-south dichotomy, among others, peace would reign! Before you think I am talking only about the world, look at your relationships in your house, your family, your neighborhood, and your workplace. See if Christ's love has destroyed your barriers or if you still live in fear! *Let love in you build your relationships for peace!*

- Faith in God means trusting Him to fight your battles. One could argue that God gives wisdom for weapons to be produced. Yet, God reduced the size of David's army, and they hardly used any spears in many of their wars. Jericho's walls were brought down by worship, not weapons. God knows the future and has told it to us. The time is coming when all of these tanks, war aircraft and ships, and other weapons shall be melted off into development tools. God will take charge of His world He created and,

"He will judge between many peoples and will settle disputes for strong nations far and wide. They will beat their swords into plowshares and their spears into pruning hooks. Nation will not take up sword against nation, nor will they train for war anymore" (Micah 4:3, NIV).

Beloved in the Lord, not one word of what God gave as prophecies has ever failed. All will be fulfilled. Trust in the Lord. Do not fear man, love him. Do not be intimidated by bullies, trust God. He is your safety. He will fight for you. He will give you peace, bless you, and cause you to be a blessing even to your enemies, in Jesus' Name.

APPRECIATE YOUR LIFE: IT WAS PAID FOR!

"I appreciate every new day, no matter the nature of the weather outside," said one of those celebrating his survival from the Vietnam War during Memorial Day in the United States. He is one of those who narrowly escaped death at one of America's worst wars in which 58,220 American soldiers died. The war ended over fifty years ago, but when those who took part in it talk, it is as if it was just yesterday. War is bad, surviving is memorable, and appreciation of it is a good thing. My sister escaped from the town of Kumbo (Cameroon) during the most dangerous time of the Anglophone civil struggle, and she had lost weight considerably. In her words, "On fierce fighting days, bullets were falling on our roof like heavy rain." Just the thought of going back to that town drives her nuts. On the other hand, the Vietnamese hardly talk about the war, although about two million Vietnamese civilians and between 200,000 and 250,000 South Vietnamese soldiers died.

A TV station in Cameroon aired a report about a sister who had lost most family members, especially her siblings. Death followed a trip to the village land for each of them and/or their spouse. She lives in fear and uncertainty, wondering what is in that land that has killed the parents and now her brothers and sisters. Their war is invisible, but the casualties are physical.

Beloved, Jesus went to the cross to fight the invisible war for you, so that you can live an appreciative life of victory without fear and in faith, build a legacy and influence lives for good.

"When you were dead in your sins and in the uncircumcision of your flesh, God made you alive with Christ. He forgave us all our sins,...And having disarmed the powers and authorities, he made a public spectacle of them, triumphing over them by the cross" (Colossians 2:13, 15, NIV).

Child of God:

- Thank God for your life daily and celebrate your freedom. Each day is a gift for you, no matter how things might go out there. Being worried does not change situations, but being appreciative gives you a different outlook despite the difficulties you may face.

- Whatever happens to you, remember that God loves you. You do not only matter; you are precious to Him. That is why Jesus took your place on the cross. Out of love, **"You were bought at a price" (1 Corinthians 6:20b NIV).**

- Pray against hostilities and wars. No matter the level, war or conflict wastes lives, frustrates people and delays development. Ask God to enable people in conflict situations to sit down and talk, and negotiate it to the end, so their children will not bear the consequences.

- Check yourself and deal with any conflicting situation at your individual, family, or community level. *Never allow or make way for your children to inherit your wars or live the consequences of your battles.*

"If it is possible, as far as it depends on you, live at peace with everyone" (Romans 12:18 NIV). And, "The God of peace [will] be with you..." (Romans 15:33 NIV) in Jesus' Name.

SHALOM (PEACE)

The disciples were seated with worried hearts, not yet sure what to do given that their Master had died. They were not sure what the Jewish leaders would do to them in the absence of Jesus, so they were afraid. They had their door locked as they sat inside. Yes, they heard He had resurrected but were not yet able to make meaning out of it. In fact, Thomas was not yet convinced that the story about His resurrection was true. Jesus appeared to them and told them, **"...Peace be with you" (John 20:26, NIV).** What a relief they must have had! War brings worries and an absence of peace. Hunger and other difficulties also bring fear and a lack of peace. But uncertainty about the future is a major source of fear and lack of peace.

I prepared for my high school exams, the Advance Level General Certificate of Education, with much uncertainty in my mind. Indeed, my friend and I were studying very hard, but we saw others who studied much more than us. When we got to the school and realized that we had not reviewed as many past questions as they had done, our fear increased. Also, I had believed that I would go to university in Nigeria, thereby, escaping the French language that caused enormous frustration to English speaking students at the nation's only and French language-dominated university in Yaoundé. But as I was preparing for the exams, my parents were clear that they did not have money for me to go to Yaoundé, let alone Nigeria. All the same, I wrote the exam with little hope.

Two months later, there was joy in our family when my name was read on the National Radio as successful. For a week or so, I was between happy and sad as we sat there having no idea what the next step for me would be. As God would have it, an uncle came home for his holiday. My parents went and told him about my success and their difficulty. The month ended with me in the elitist, government officials' residential area in Yaoundé, attending the University of Yaoundé. Of course, I faced the French with tears (another long story), but today, all of that is history. I even do my lectures at the faculty in French, hahaha! Uncertainty can cripple one's energy and peace if the focus is on the stress factors involved.

Beloved in the Lord, Jesus knew the world He had lived in and that He was leaving His disciples in was a tough place in which to be. He gave them this peace formula:

"Peace I leave with you; my peace I give you. I do not give to you as the world gives. Do not let your hearts be troubled and do not be afraid...." and **"I have told you these things, so that in me you may have peace. In this world you will have trouble. But take heart! I have overcome the world" (John 14:27; 16:33, NIV).**

Whatever you are going through or whatever the future holds for you, dear friend, do not be afraid. It does not matter how many stress factors you can count for yourself; even if you are not well prepared for the exams or the discussions about your business, or for the job interview you have; despite the magnitude of the uncertainties for your future or those of your children, do not be

53

afraid. Jesus says you should take heart and trust in Him. Believe in Him because God works through Him, and He is your Intercessor. He made you. He is taking care of you and yours. He holds your future, and it will be well. Keep focused on Him and move on. It shall be well with you and yours, in Jesus' Name. *Shalom, Shalom.*

STRIVE TO STAND FIRM TO THE END!

When one is young, he or she hardly thinks about death. Also, when one is popular or successful in life, death seems like an illusion, not a reality. But a day comes when all battles against death are lost, and those left behind have their eyes filled with tears, their hearts broken, and their minds filled with questions that never get satisfactory answers. Death always takes us by surprise, even when we know that someone is sick and will most likely die. That all shall die is a truth from which no one can escape. The reality we can choose is what to do and where to stand at death, in terms of work and spirituality.

The eyes of many Cameroonians were filled with tears as a great man, a great name, and a great actor in the political landscape of the nation, followed Italian Berlusconi to the world beyond. Ni John Fru Ndi was a great political icon who led the nation to multiparty politics when he launched the Social Democratic Front (SDF) party in 1990. He was a great source of hope, especially for the Anglophones who felt marginalized and saw the SDF as the answer to their prayer. He and the party gained national acclaim and became the leading political party in the nation. In fact, the SDF was such a great opposition party that the near disappearance of this force in the present political dispensation has made some commentators say that Cameroon is back to a one-party state, though with over two hundred legalized parties.

Cameroonians wept for Fru Ndi but had a major question: What happened? No! Not what happened that he died, but what happened that His Excellency Fru Ndi left the SDF in factions, with many of the main personalities of the party gone, away from the party or dead? What happened that though many people within the party called for him to step down as the leader of the party, he remained there and only announced that he would step down a few weeks before his death? What happened that he rather seemed to have become a friend of the government party, the Cameroon Peoples' Democratic Movement (CPDM)? What happened that some of his party militants took him to court and were subsequently dismissed from the party? What happened that the party he has left behind has many scandals? What happened that SDF returned Cameroon to a one-party state, such that the government won all senate seats, giving six (of the appointed seats) to "opposition parties" with famous but now infamous SDF reserving one senate seat as an appointment from the president, not elected? The story of Pa Fru Ndi and the SDF reminds me of one Biblical verse, **"So, if you think you are standing firm, be careful that you don't fall" (1 Corinthians 10:12, NIV)**! Be careful!

Beloved in the Lord, in all works of life and much more seriously, in our spiritual walk with God, temptations come in various forms because the enemy is always at work. The various battles Fru Ndi and the SDF fought in and out of the party, the frustrations from their failures and stolen victories, the invitations from the corrupt, bribe stricken political arena, and the failure to bring fresh blood and fresh political minds to the leadership of the party, were all trials and temptations that immobilized Fru Ndi and the SDF in the last few years. It led almost to the burial of the party that awaited the burial of its founding father. Dear friend, in your walk with God and in your work in the professional and sociopolitical and economic world, stand firm to the end. Difficulties shall prevail but hold unto the Lord for,

"No temptation has overtaken you except what is common to mankind. And God is faithful; he will not let you be tempted beyond what you can bear. But when you are tempted, he will also provide a way out so that you can endure it" (1 Corinthians 10:13, NIV).

When the Lord comes, for you or for the world, may He find faith in you, in Jesus' Name.

MORALITY IN THE WORLD THAT IGNORES GOD!

So much is changing in the world today that is honestly making the world frightening. Sometimes, one wonders why it is so hard to learn from history, but when so much attention is given to emotional satisfaction, people neither care about what history teaches nor even have time for history lessons. We are in a world where people are fully happy when they have food on the table and can enjoy themselves in whatever way, regardless of what happens to those around them.

Ah, somehow, I was taken by surprise when it was announced that the most influential politician in the history of Italy, Silvio Berlusconi was dead. He was so popular and so influential that one could hardly miss his stories. He had been Italian Prime Minister three times within thirty years. One journalist described him as "a politician, a billionaire, a womanizer and a convicted fraudster." Another added that he was a buffoon and a racist. That Berlusconi was not convicted and imprisoned does not mean he was not guilty of paying for and having sex with an underage, seventeen-year-old girl. He was convicted of fraud, dismissed from the senate and asked to do community labor. Yet, while Italy was looking for a moral compass for the next generation, Berlusconi, at 85, was talking of running for presidency. Death stopped him! What morality would he have brought to that office? Do we not have a moral crisis?

United States president, Joe Biden, at the White House, celebrated Pride Month in honor and favor of transgender people. Such open and clear support for homosexuality and sexual confusion may be politically right in this season of politics for popularity, rather than politics for values, but where does it lead the people? My fear is that it is leading the world on the highway lane back to Sodom and Gomorrah. God loved the people, but their immorality had gotten to an alarming popular level. Abraham pleaded with God to spare the cities for the sake of the righteous; **"Then he said, "May the Lord not be angry, but let me speak just once more. What if only ten can be found there?" He answered, "For the sake of ten, I will not destroy it" (Genesis 18:32, NIV).** Sadly, there were not even ten people in Sodom who had their morality in check!

Beloved, in this world of fallen morality, you can be different. Be like Lot. When the angels of destruction came into the city, Lot saw them as ordinary men. He housed them for the night, keeping them away from the rapists who preferred men to women. He fought hard to protect them. The next morning, the angels told him to take his family away. He was hesitating.

"When he hesitated, the men [angels] grasped his hand and the hands of his wife and of his two daughters and led them safely out of the city, for the Lord was merciful to them. As soon as they had brought them out, one of them said, "Flee for your lives! Don't look back, and don't stop anywhere in the plain! Flee to the mountains or you will be swept away" (Genesis 19:16-17, NIV)!

Lot and his daughters were saved. May the Lord grant you grace to trust Him and remain faithful to Him through your faith in Christ Jesus. In that way, if His wrath falls on our world, God will spare you. In our morally well-decayed world, **"Do not follow the crowd in doing wrong" (Exodus 23:2a, NIV).** Then you will be blessed and be a blessing to many others, in Jesus' Name.

WITH YOUR POWER, BUILD OTHERS!

The race for the presidency of the United States of America in 2024 was on. Florida Governor Ron DeSantis announced his entrance into the race, and beside him was one of the world's richest people and owner of Twitter, Elon Musk. Interestingly, his announcement had technical problems and did not get off to a good start. Economic, technical and political power combined could still fail. DeSantis had wealthy people in his state promising to support him in his race for the White House. But money may not have been enough, in spite of the campaigns and advertisements he could purchase. Obama raised little and big amounts from all classes of income earners, mostly at the individual level, to run the campaign for his presidential race in 2008. It is easy to interpret the high political power accompanied by the rich as a move to enrich themselves and do more for themselves than for the people. In Africa, the poor do not generally contribute financially to election campaigns because they are rather bribed to vote for the highest bidder for their votes. When the corrupters get to power, they do very little, if anything, for the people. It is easy for power to concentrate on personal gains and selfish ends, but it is better when power seeks the good of others.

One can understand God's perspective of power by noting that Jesus did not allow the Jews to physically make Him their king. They saw His power in the miracles He did and thought they had gotten one who would deliver them from the hands of the Roman colonizers. They even attempted to make Him king.

"After the people saw the sign Jesus performed, they began to say, "Surely this is the Prophet who is to come into the world." Jesus, knowing that they intended to come and make him king by force, withdrew again to a mountain by himself" (John 6:14-15, NIV).

When Jesus withdrew, He started giving them very tough lessons on individual living. Most of the people departed from Him because of the difficulty of His teaching. God's focus is our individual transformation and commitment to sacrificial living. Only in that commitment can one be sure that when he or she gets power, it will be for the common good. Jesus would not be King on the physical throne of the Jews because He was the King of all the earth, and because His assignment was to give us individual freedom, spiritually.

- When you plan your future, be certain it will be for success. To what end? For what good? Think beyond yourself and your children. See yourself gaining economic power to employ more people and change their lives for good. See yourself getting into politics, not just to become a great name but to bring growth and development to your nation and beyond. Do not just write academic papers, write transformational papers in your area of studies, and aim to transform by it.

- If you hold any form of power now, what is it doing to you? At whatever level in whatever organization in which you take part (including a social group, village, or political group), how is your power making a difference? Remember that only one thing will make your name memorable in history. The same one thing will give you a reward in heaven: the good deeds you would have done for others. No one talks about the number of cars, houses, farms, or amount(s) of money in the bank account(s) of the person being buried. It is always about what the man had done. **"Then I heard a voice from heaven say, "Write this: Blessed are the dead who die in the Lord from now on." "Yes," says the Spirit, "they will rest from their labor, for their deeds will follow them" (Revelation 14:13, NIV).**

With all the abilities God gives you, ensure that good deeds shall follow you heavenward, then both heaven and earth shall celebrate your life, in Jesus' Name.

YOUR FUTURE: RESULT OR CHANCE?

It was a great Friday evening as I sat in front of the TV and saw Senegal carry the day. It was a wonderful conclusion to the football season. They won all the football competitions at the African level in the 2022-2023 football season. I wonder if any nation has done that at any time in history. It is a remarkable record. Most football analysts see this as the result of about ten years of hard work and conscious investment in the sector. Considering that the nation has the best teams in Africa in all age groups, one can expect Senegal to shine bright in African football in the years to come.

However, as I saw the under seventeen-year-old teenagers jumping around and celebrating their victory, I could not help thinking about the political upheavals at home, with their president almost poised to run for a third term, thus, raising dust in the nation. While the opposition argued that the constitution was clear that one cannot run for more than two terms, President Macky Sall said the constitutional council considered his first term to be outside the scope of the reform that changed terms from seven to five years in 2016 while he was in his first term. In 2024, he would have been sixty-three years old and president for twelve years and. The next day, Saturday (May 20th) Cameroon was celebrating its National Day, and some youths were alleged to have called for President Paul Biya, longest reigning president and visibly exhausted, to stand again in the next presidential elections. Ah! What if these elders who have served their nations well gave way to the young and coached them to glorious victories? It took a retired footballer to coach and bring such change in the football sector in Senegal. Should the political sector not learn from that, oh African?

David ruled at the time of the monarchy. Yet, he appointed Solomon, his son, as regent. Solomon started his reign when his father was still alive, and it was David's joy. When he made Solomon king, the royal officials came and congratulated King David, saying,

"…'May your God make Solomon's name more famous than yours and his throne greater than yours!' And the king bowed in worship on his bed and said, 'Praise be to the Lord, the God of Israel, who has allowed my eyes to see success on my throne today'" (1 Kings 1:47-48, NIV).

David had the time to give good counsel and guidance to King Solomon before he died. Succession is a beautiful thing when well prepared and managed.

Beloved in the Lord:

- Do not take your future for granted. Success needs planning *with the Lord.*

- Do not just assume that your children's future will be fine. Plan and do something about it.

- Young friend, invest in your future. Do not eat the little you have now and struggle with the years to come. Work towards a good future. Work hard!

- Pray for your leaders. Ask God to give them the wisdom to invest in the future of your village, community or nation. Ask God to help them know when to quit the stage and become coaches to the younger ones who are energetic and intelligent. Do not leave your future in the hands of chance; work for its results and the Lord will be with you, in Jesus' Name.

HELP THOSE IN AUTHORITY

Managing power and service is a very delicate and difficult balance to strike. I supervised a thesis on church leadership, specifically in the relationship between trained pastors and lay leadership in the church. When I read it, I realized that the serious problems I had lived, managed, and sometimes been badly wounded by, are happening in other nations and Christian denominations. In spite of the more clearly divine nature of church leadership, there is a human tendency to grab and hold onto undue power in church, not for the common good but for personal pride and access to destructive authority. If this is so in the church, it cannot be easier in society where self is more at play than in the church.

At his coronation, King Charles III was given authority over the nation, the British Oversees Territories, and at least symbolically, over the Commonwealth of Nations. But he was told that the sword they put in his hand was the sword of mercy not of might and is a sword of justice not judgment. He was given a scepter and told it was for kingly power of justice, equality and peace. He was given a glove to remind him that he should be gentle in exercising power. How can one be humble and gentle when over five thousand soldiers from all over his territories and the Commonwealth of Nations escorted him to and from the church, reminding him of the level of security he has and the power with which he can defend the monarchy? We have seen and experienced civilian dictatorships oiled by the commander of the armed forces' ability to use the army against the freedoms of the people for selfish gains. In the U.S. presidential elections which Donald Trump won, I remember a Democrat who was campaigning against him asking how reasonable it was for a man like Trump to have the right to decide if there could be a nuclear war. Presidential decisions are delicate and dangerous, and presidential protection by power and the constitution can easily promote an abuse of power. It takes God and grace to keep things checked, to keep the leaders' hearts from selfishness and evil, and encouraged to selflessly fight for the good of the people. It takes God for those in power to see the opposition as contributors for the public good rather than people struggling to steal their buttered bread. It takes God and grace for leaders to respect their terms of office, keep the constitution, and be servants when they come from traditions where authority is hereditary and for life. There are very few nations like Britain where the prime minister can be voted out of office or made to resign after less than two months in office. Even so, that has happened only once in British history. The balance between power and service is a difficult pendulum to swing into equilibrium.

Beloved in the Lord Jesus, it boils down to the individual heart. That is why one can hear passion in Paul's pen when he calls on us,

"I urge, then, first of all, that petitions, prayers, intercession and thanksgiving be made for all people - for kings and all those in authority, that we may live peaceful and quiet lives in all godliness and holiness. For there is one God and one

mediator between God and mankind, the man Christ Jesus" (1 Timothy 2:1-2, 5, NIV).

Two things:

- We ought to pray without getting tired because it comes down to the individual heart. **"Righteousness exalts a nation, but sin condemns any people" (Proverbs 14:34, NIV).** Yes, but this righteousness is the righteousness of the nation who should let God rule, and the hearts of the led who should choose leaders without fear or favor but in good evaluation of their intents. Pray!

- We ought to speak the truth to leaders when we have the opportunity. It is bad when people pray, fold their arms, and wait for angels to come and correct or rebuke leaders the way Jesus and John the Baptist did. Only days after the coronation, the archbishop who coronated the king spoke publicly against King Charles III over the decision to send refugees to Rwanda. Christian, speak the truth, condemn evil, and point out error and selfishness to your leaders. Get to parliament, political parties, and speak for change. Go to family meetings and church meetings and speak with humility, love, and firmness. Go to the individual leaders when God gives you grace and call them to order in their chambers. Speak!

Oh, that God would give us the hearts of gold, the mouths of Jesus and John the Baptist, and the hands of Aaron and Hur (Exodus 17:12), to love our leaders, speak truth to them, and uphold them when they are right! That is the highway to good governance at all levels and in all societies. That is the highway to our being blessed as a people. That is the highway to a secure future for our children. Do not be passive towards leadership: *pray, speak, uphold,* in Jesus' Name.

IT IS A BLESSING TO SERVE!

I was a young boy of about twelve when my sister with whom I went to the farm alongside my mother was made a female chief in the village. The immediate consequence was that she stopped going to the farm and stayed in the palace. We lost our partner at the farm, not to death but to leadership. She brought some goodness to the village but not to us as her immediate family. This event ran past my mind last Saturday as I watched King Charles III's welcome into the church for the coronation. He was welcomed by a child about the age I was at my sister's enthronement. The boy came before the king and told him, "As children of the kingdom, we welcome you in the name of the King of Kings." The King's response was, "I come to serve." The idea of service ran through the coronation exercise, and no one who was there or who watched it could fail to notice this theme of service that dominated throughout. The sermon crowned it all when the preacher described service as, "The aim of all righteous governments." Yes!

We often quote the Bible where it says that people in authority are placed there by God, but we often miss the objective stated in the text. God says rulers are in authority: **"... to punish those who do wrong and to commend those who do right" (1 Peter 2:14b, NIV).** Seated in that cathedral at Westminster there were representatives of some of the very corrupt governments on earth. I wonder what this strong call to service meant to them. I wonder if they heard this archbishop's definition of the aim of righteous government. But then, do these unrighteous, corrupt governments hide the fact that they are corrupt? Well, this serviceless, unrighteous culture is learned at a young age.

As I said before, my young sister was taken from the farm and given leadership responsibility and farm work stopped for her. She was not paid a salary. Yet, someone had to feed her. Who? With food from where? In contrast, the Monday after the coronation, the British public and the British royal family, including the grandchildren of the just coronated king, were out to do voluntary service in their various communities. Ah, the sight of it was beautiful.

Some years back, as we left the church yard early in the morning to go and dance into the church in celebration of the resurrection, I realized that it had rained and the road was muddy with stagnant water too, making passage difficult. I went back to the house, got a spade, came and cleared the mud and directed the rainwater off the road while the Christians danced in the streets on their way to church. I missed the celebration but was quite happy that morning. Interestingly, some Christians did not find it funny that I was not dancing with the people! Beloved in the Lord, we can serve and teach our children to grow as servants, not lords. If in everything you are called to do, you think beyond what you will benefit, to what others will gain from you, you can be a servant and enjoy it as well as be blessed by it as you bless others. **"Each of you should** use whatever gift you have received to serve others, as faithful stewards of God's grace in its various forms" (1 Peter 4:10, NIV). That is the way to grow a society! Please, serve, in Jesus' Name.

BE AT PEACE, YOUR KING REIGNS!

I was among the 18.8 million people who tuned in to watch the coronation of the British monarch, King Charles III. It was a rich event; colorful, historic, quite religious and very well attended. The British Overseas Territories were well represented, and their flags were displayed as the representatives of each territory walked into the church for the event. These territories are the fourteen with a constitutional and historical link with the United Kingdom. They are the last remnants of the former British Empire and do not form part of the United Kingdom itself but remind us of the fact that the United Kingdom once controlled a huge part of the world's population as a colonial power. Of course, things have changed, and King Charles III takes over in a different world than in colonial days.

The event was also full of symbolism. Along with the crown on His head, the king was given many objects whose meaning or symbolism were explained as they handed over the objects to him. One that caught my attention in surprise was the orb, an oval object that looked like a globe with a cross above it. The king took it and held it in his hand. It represents the Christian world. In handing it to the king, he was reminded that, **"The kingdom of this world has become the kingdom of our Lord and of His Messiah..."** **(Revelation 11:15)**. This is surely from the colonial days when the King of England controlled much of the world. The cross on this orb reminds the king that his rule must submit to the leadership of

Jesus and the work on the cross. What English kings did in those days in colonial Africa and India among others did not show that this submission to Jesus was important to them. King Charles III has no global jurisdiction. He rules Great Britain under a constitution, influences the British Oversees Territories, and enjoys a respect as Head of the Commonwealth. He is not really my king and may not be yours if you are not British.

Beloved in the Lord, the good news is that we have a King who does not make errors, whose power is not limited, and who does not need to be reminded of the need for humility and righteousness. Whatever you are going through now, however you may feel oppressed now, relax. Jesus is your conquering King. The time is coming when the words of heavenly praise and worship shall become a reality in its fullness.

"The seventh angel sounded his trumpet, and there were loud voices in heaven, which said: 'The kingdom of the world has become the kingdom of our Lord and of his Messiah, and he will reign for ever and ever.' And the twenty-four elders, who were seated on their thrones before God, fell on their faces and worshiped God, saying: "We give thanks to you, Lord God Almighty, the One who is and who was, because you have taken your great power and have begun to reign" (Revelation 11:15-17, NIV).

Do not just look forward to when all kings and rulers of the earth shall submit to Christ. Look up to Jesus, our Messiah. He is your King and has won your battles for you. Now, you just have to follow Him, live in victory, and trust Him in any situation and with every difficulty you have. Your King reigns for your blessings and life. May He guide all of your affairs, in Jesus' Name.

THE PARADOX OF SELF-SURRENDER

The nation of Sudan was supposed to be handed over to a civilian government by the end of 2023, but in April 15, 2023 that nation was experiencing a very deadly war between the two main military leaders in the nation. The cause of this can be traced into history and the difficulty of integrating the Rapid Support Forces (RSF) into the regular army. The reality goes down to the personal level where neither of the two leaders were willing to give up power and hand the nation to civilian rule. In eleven days, there were more than 3,700 women, men or children wounded, with over 420 killed in the conflict. This included 264 civilians. Thousands fled in different directions in search of safety. Many nations evacuated their nationals, including medical staff, from Sudan. The nation was being destroyed because of the unwillingness of self-surrender. Two people, unwilling to lay down their power, were ready to sacrifice a whole nation. They did not understand the paradox of self-sacrifice! They are not the only ones. There are many such fights in our families, villages, and even in the church.

Jesus told His disciples and, therefore, us, **"Remember Lot's wife! Whoever tries to keep their life will lose it, and whoever loses their life will preserve it" (Luke 17:32-33, NIV).** Lot's wife became a pillar of salt for looking back at the time they were escaping Sodom and Gomorrah. Because they looked back to when they enjoyed power, General Abdel Fattah al-Burhan (leading the ruling council) and his assistant, General Mohammed Hamdan

Dagalo, plunged the nation into a journey back into darkness, depravity and death. But Jesus said that the best way they could have their power, comfort, and popularity would have been to give up their self-desires for the sake of the nation. If they both did, and the nation returned to civilian rule as planned, they would be highly respected, honored, taken care of, and thousands of people who were on the run would have been there to sing their praises. Whoever gives up the pleasures and promotion of self, for the sake of Christ's Kingdom, receives a divine reward.

"To the person who pleases him, God gives wisdom, knowledge and happiness, but to the sinner he gives the task of gathering and storing up wealth to hand it over to the one who pleases God. This too is meaningless, a chasing after the wind" (Ecclesiastes 2:26, NIV).

Child of God, whatever God is asking you to sacrifice for the children around you, your family, your church, your neighborhood or your nation, just surrender. It may be great and painful but remember that it is a paradox. At first you lose in surrender and feel initial pain, but the reward God will give you here and in the age to come will greatly outweigh the pain. Jesus endured the cross and got a Name that is higher than every other name. In small things as in big things, live a life of self-surrender and you shall be a great blessing to your generation and shall be blessed as well, in Jesus' Name.

CULTURES:
DIVINE DISUNITY OR HUMAN DIVERSITY?

What could have caused five "white" women and one "white" man (six) have a "black" girl badly beaten outside of London? Issues of race and cultural differences remain a volatile subject that is hardly brought to total submission to love and honor. My uncle attended school in America in the 1970s and left the church because of open discrimination against his color. Today, in that country, there are "white people" who literarily move out of communities and buy houses elsewhere when they realize that people of African, Asian or Latino origins have moved into their neighborhood. My country is bicultural, bijudicial and bilingual. While the multicultural mix is celebrated politically, the reality on the ground is quite worrying, and actual unity is hard. I stood almost helplessly in a class I teach, when pastor-students of one language expression shouted at a person to do his presentation in "their language" despite the official bilingual policy of the school. The challenges of multiculturalism as a jewel for which we should have pride in the globalized world is huge.

To understand the measure of challenges involved, it is good to get back to the origin(s). How did language differences come about?

"Now the whole world had one language and a common speech. Then they said, 'Come, let us build ourselves a city, with a tower that reaches to the heavens, so that we may make a name for ourselves; otherwise we will be scattered over the face of the whole earth.' The Lord said, 'If as one people speaking the same language they have begun to do this, then

nothing they plan to do will be impossible for them. Come, let us go down and confuse their language so they will not understand each other.' So the Lord scattered them from there over all the earth, and they stopped building the city. That is why it was called Babel - because there the Lord confused the language of the whole world. From there the Lord scattered them over the face of the whole earth" (Genesis 11:1, 4, 6-9, NIV).

- Before Babel the world had one language.

- Then, they began building a tower to make a name for themselves!

- They wanted to keep themselves from being scattered over the earth.

- But God confused their language and scattered them all over the earth, isolated from each other by language. Culture, of which language is part, was God's way of creating a disunity which He would Himself solve in Christ. Human effort to unite in diversity is a daunting task. The individual defends his personality; the family defends their heritage; and the cultural entity (tribe) defends its identity. It is hard to unite at these different levels. It is even worse to keep away pride and unite in diversity at the highest level of a nation.

Beloved in The Lord, it is only in Christ that we are told, **"Here there is no Gentile or Jew, circumcised or uncircumcised, barbarian, Scythian, slave or free, but Christ is all, and is in all" (Colossians 3:11, NIV).** Without Christ, unity is hard. It is the death of Christ that broke the dividing wall to make people of divergent cultures one. Therefore:

- Friendship, including marriage that is cross-cultural will only be at peace if those involved fear God and allow the Holy Spirit to bring them together.

- In a multicultural church, Christ must be first in all things to keep the cultures from splitting Christ's body.

- If multiculturalism would be an asset in our society, we must cry out for honest validation with a Christ-centered character. **"Therefore, as God's chosen people, holy and dearly loved, clothe yourselves with compassion, kindness, humility, gentleness and patience" (Colossians 3:12, NIV).**

May your identity as a child of God be most important to you so you will be a factor of unity wherever you are or will be, in Jesus' Name.

GOODNESS IN AN EVIL WORLD!

One of the most difficult things God demands in the Bible is that we should overcome evil in the world with good. That does not sound meaningful to a heightened and proud mind but makes much sense for one who really wants peace. The world passed through a tough period of competition between the great powers, where there was much suspicion and spying on each other. Espionage was big but when the nations addressed it and built relationships of trust and communion among themselves, the Cold War ended. But somehow, suspicious behavior started again among them and eventually, the arms race became a known reality where each superpower tried to beat the rest in the superiority of their weapons. The war in Ukraine is or was a test of that superiority. Overcoming evil with good is not a thought that can find support where it might be argued that doing good to a wicked enemy will be seen as weakness. Sad!

One could read the attempt by President Donald Trump to relate and discuss with North Korea as an attempt to be good to an "evil person." Just for him to go twenty steps into this well-walled nation, the greatest Hermit Kingdom on earth, was historic. Yet, for almost the first time in history, a North Korean president was happy with a U.S. president and expressed he was "overjoyed" at the meeting. It is so hard to do good to an evil person because it looks worthless. It is risk-taking; it takes grace and trust in God to do that. Yet, it is the best road to a meaningful win-win relationship that provides for safety and comfort for both parties. How I pray that someday the world will change from, "If you want peace build an army" to "If you want peace build relationships in good deeds!"

Beloved in the Lord, do you have some evil people around you? Are there some friends, co-workers, or even relations between whom things are extremely bad? Yes, **"...If your enemy is hungry, feed him; if he is thirsty, give him something to drink. In doing this, you will heap burning coals on his head"** **(Romans 12:20, NIV).** Do not wait for your enemy to be hungry or thirsty because you may be seen as coming in strength to fill a gap and claim having done it. Rather than waiting, seek and exploit opportunities to do good to enemies, evil or wicked people because the Lord has commanded it. If you do good, that goodness could overcome evil beyond your greatest imagination. So, **"Do not be overcome by evil, but overcome evil with good" (Romans 12:21, NIV)** and God will bless you greatly and use you to bless others mightily, in Jesus' Name.

IN A GOOD COURSE, GOD IS WITH YOU!

I had never tried to find out how old Martin Luther King Jr. was by the time he died. It was as if the fact that he was killed in 1968 informed my brain that he died at 68. But, as I prepared to attend a birthday party, I decided to research a little on him only to discover that he died at thirty-nine. At that age, he was already an international figure, actively involved in the Civil Rights Movement. Then, Jaylen Smith was one of the youngest mayors in U.S. history (world history I believe). He was elected mayor of Earle, Arkansas at the age of eighteen and had only finished high school. You see, fighting a good course is not about age or experience but determination, some knowledge, and the presence of God. When God is with you, you can do great things and go far in a course.

Jesus' public ministry lasted three years and He died at the age of about thirty. David became the king of Israel at age thirty. He had already proven the presence of God with him by killing a lion and a bear with his bare hands and by killing the Philistine's giant Goliath with a stone from a sling. David, Jesus, and Martin Luther King Jr. were not just fighting a good course; they were fighting a God course. All of them had great opposition to their course. David faced serious opposition from his elder brothers when he wanted to face Goliath and a serious threat from the king who wanted to kill him at all costs. Jesus was opposed all the way and was crucified as a criminal without a crime. MLK was shot dead for the good of the nation, not just her citizens of African origin. Fear did not stop any of them in their fight and threats did not stop them from accomplishing their purposes. David said it for them all and for you and I, as we face a hostile world and pursue a course for God's glory, confessing: **"I love you, Lord, my strength. The Lord is my rock, my fortress and my deliverer; my God is my rock, in whom I take refuge, my shield and the horn of my salvation, my stronghold" (Psalm 18:1-2, NIV).**

Beloved in The Lord:

- What course are you living for or pursuing? Ensure that God is in it and remember that He is your strength.

- Age is not an issue. If God is calling you to an action for His people, no matter how little or complicated it may be, trust Him and go for it. Let fear and threat not stop you.

- Do not waste your youthful age! History is not for the old but for the determined and prepared. May you be remembered for what you did for your people, God's people and the world, not by how long you lived!

- If you are elderly, and God used you most in your old age, do not block the way for the young! Mentor them and give them the opportunity for God to use them and let His people gain from the strength of their youth. There is no gain in being a living and inactive "acting" ancestor in a struggling family or world with vibrant, energetic and intelligent youths.

Beloved in the Lord, the good fight of life and faith is empowered and accompanied by God. In all you do, focus on the needs of the people and God's presence with you. Fight the good, God fight. One of these days you will be so blessed, bless others and eventually hear from God "Welcome home good and faithful servant. Come and share your Master's happiness," in Jesus' Name.

JESUS KNOWS YOUR CULTURE: TRUST HIM!

A few years ago, two of us from Cameroon attended the Washington National Prayer Breakfast that brought together political leaders from over a hundred nations. Most of the people were dressed in suits but there were a few who dressed in traditional regalia, from India for example. But the Northwest Cameroon regalia we wore caught the attention of many. Yes, we celebrated culture; it's richness and diversity within the family of one great God who made Himself known to us through Christ our Lord. I have seen this scene numerous times, where in terms of clothing, cultural diversity is enjoyed and shared. However, when we get into the inner elements of culture such as the traditions that influence values and behaviors, collaboration becomes a big issue. Yet, Jesus knows it all!

We only have a glimpse of heaven from what the Bible tells us; yet the little we know of heaven tells us that it was a great sacrifice for Christ to leave that awesomeness to come and suffer with humanity. Why did He do that? To experience our struggle and be able to help us.

"Son though he was, he learned obedience from what he suffered and, once made perfect, he became the source of eternal salvation for all who obey him and was designated by God to be high priest in the order of Melchizedek" (Hebrews 5:8-10, NIV).

Jesus was born and He grew up in the Greco-Roman world. God could have sent Him down when Israel was young and single in "culture" but instead He sent Christ at the time that the globalization of the time, dominated by Greek and Roman civilizations and cultures, was at its apex. Jesus experienced and understood the mix of human responses to its biophysical environment: culture. He experienced the pain of colonialism (Israel oppressed by Rome). He lived the pain of discrimination involving gender issues (woman with the issue of blood). He handled racial issues (Samaritan woman) and bore the agony of religious discrimination (the pain of a Pharisaic God-ness without godliness) which led to His own death. Nothing in the present world is strange to Him.

Yet, He did not fight any of these physical, political, and cultural realities. Peacebuilding scientists tell us that conflict issues that involve structural and cultural challenges and concerns are tough to solve. However, Jesus concentrated on what was tougher - the battle within, with *sin*! Unless God cleanses humanity of sin, the desperate nature of the human heart can only make conflicts from value differences very insurmountable.

Beloved in the Lord, deliverance from sin is the one thing needed for you to have a great family, to have great tribal relationships and to break the neck of tribal and racial tensions. As long as sin stands tall in our hearts, there is no "living together," and no benefits of cultural diversity. If you would make the most of your culture in order to understand its usefulness and sift it of human error to leave the best of it for you and others, Christ must reign first in your heart. Through faith in the Lord Jesus Christ, let God make room for you in heaven; let Him also make you an instrument of goodness within your culture, and give you the best of your culture, in Jesus' Name.

YOUTH: WORSHIP THE LORD OF YOUR FUTURE

We were excited, trekking for about two hours, as children in primary school, to go celebrate National Youth Day. Honestly, I am not sure that we understood what we celebrated. At the celebration, after the match ended, we ate and played, watched traditional dances and cheered the sports team from our school. Then, it was time for another long trek that got us home way after sunset. The problem is, I still am not sure if I really understand what the Youth Day celebration in my nation, even today, is all about.

It is hard for young people to keep celebrating the prospects of their future in a country where a youth is seemingly defined as anyone who is alive. People who have long passed their retirement age are still sitting in offices while actual youth roam the streets unemployed despite having diplomas and degrees as high as PhD. Yes, the youth can be blamed for laziness but how many industries are there without workers because youth are lazy? Young people will walk past officials on National Youth Day in the heat of the dry season sun. Meanwhile the state officials wait anxiously for the ceremony to end so they can go and celebrate Youth Day in the official residence of administrators, with money that could pay the salaries of more than a few young people. When a handful of youths get crumbs from under the table of the wicked, they hail their crumb-givers in the loudest voice. How else can we understand that a criminal is behind bars, and some youth carry placards in public saying, "Fighting Amougou Belinga is killing the youths?" If the youth do not eat the bread of justice and hard work; whoever is to blame will bear the wrath of the All Mighty who sends leaders, **"... to punish those who do wrong and to commend those who do right" (1 Peter 2:14, NIV).**

Beloved youth, The Lord loves you and cares about your future. In any and every situation, remember, **"There is a time for everything, and a season for every activity under the heavens: a time to weep and a time to laugh, a time to mourn and a time to dance" (Ecclesiastes. 3:1 & 4, NIV).** If now is your weeping or mourning time, look up to God. His plan for you is sure and reserved for you. He has made everything beautiful in His eyes and when it is all revealed to you, you shall laugh and dance. Appreciate the elders who make your life worthwhile and give you hope. Celebrate your gracious and loving Father, God, who works out all things for your good. Indeed, your future is secured in His Hands, in Jesus' Name.

GOOD AND EVIL: HEAVEN AND HELL!

In my mind I can still see Sadam Hussein's eyes looking up from the pit where he was caught trying to run away from the soldiers who were pursuing him. It was quite pitiful. A president? Looking at soldiers from a pit, certain that he had come to the end of his road? Road to where? Not long after that, he was put to death. That sounds like his road-end, but it could not be! Another president, as hated and dreaded as Sadam, died and I remember someone calling a BBC radio program and insisting that he was praying that this former president should be kept in the hottest part of hell. You could read anger and agony in his voice. Evil is bad, especially when it has a great influence on people's lives. Evil is bad!

It is easy to attribute badness to very hideous crimes, a high level of evil. The Bible, however, is simple and straightforward on the issue. Jesus said, **"I told you that you would die in your sins; if you do not believe that I am he, you will indeed die in your sins" (John 8:24, NIV).** The emphasis is not on the type, quality or quantity of evil but simply on the reality of sin. The Bible is also clear that heaven and hell are realities. In the story of "Lazarus and the Rich Man" Jesus sounds more like He is telling a story than a parable. The transition was great for one and sorrowful for the other. **"The time came when the beggar died, and the angels carried him to Abraham's side. The rich man also died and was buried. In Hades, where he was in torment, he looked up and saw Abraham far away, with Lazarus by his side" (Luke**

16:22-23, NIV). The agony of hell is too much to be taken for a joke.

Beloved, people have argued that a God of love cannot create hell because it is too bad. They forget that God is also a God of justice. He told Adam and Eve that the day they ate of the fruit of the tree of the knowledge of good and evil, they would die. They went ahead and disobeyed, and realized that their whole life had changed, not for the better. Heaven and hell are real and are to be taken seriously. This loving God:

- Has set the terms for the execution of justice, being clear that there is a heaven for those living in righteousness and hell for those living in sin. You cannot stand before a judge and argue a ruling that is clear in the books. **"For the wages of sin is death, but the gift of God is eternal life in Christ Jesus our Lord" (Romans 6:23, NIV).** The choice is yours to make.

- He has paid the price for sin by sending His Son to the cross. Jesus was the sacrificial Lamb who came as, "**... the Lamb of God, who takes away the sin of the world" (John 1:29b, NIV)!** What more could a loving God do than give a way out of the possibility of going to hell and leaving a free will for people, each with the choice of taking the way out or not? The instruction is clear and simple, and the demand is not expensive for you and me; **"Believe in the Lord Jesus, and you will be saved - you and your household" (Acts 16:31, NIV).**

- Beloved, God loves you.

Accept that you are a sinner and believe in the death and resurrection of Jesus Christ for the forgiveness of your sins. Confess, repent and ask God to come into your heart and make you clean, acceptable to God. Ask for Him to fill your heart with His Spirit; empower you for life and prepare you for heaven. As someone has said,

Life is short.

Death is sure.

Sin the cause.

Christ the cure.

The time is now for you to accept Christ and be saved before time tells you it is too late. God loves you. Take His offer and have life for here and hereafter, in Jesus' Name.

GET THE BEST!

I grew up liking and respecting our village chief (fon) in particular and chieftaincy in general. The fon is the highest authority in the land and commands much honor. Then, I went to school and learned that "uneasy lies the head that wears the crown." There are certain painful responsibilities and consequences of top positions that are not obvious to the public eye. While respecting the highest position in the United Kingdom and the kingship, I cannot but wonder how comfortable that crown has become when the royal family is filled with scandals. King Charles III was coronated king in May 2023., still haunted by the divorce and death of Lady Diana. Her death stained the royal house as it was accused of having a hand in it. Some British citizens still have difficulties accepting Camilla as King Charles' wife. He took over a family where for the first time in history, his own child preferred leaving the royal family to gain some freedom for himself and his wife. Ah! Freedom! From what? These royal dissatisfactions: Putin's unease in Russia and the refusal of some African leaders to leave office in spite of popular discontent and obvious degradation of their nations, are telling of the fact that these high offices are not necessarily the most satisfying.

The best position, the best achievement and the best relationship in life is that which gives you the highest level of self-satisfaction or fulfillment, the greatest peace and rest. "To be loved by God is the highest relationship, the highest achievement, and the highest position in life," (Henry Blackaby)[3]. When you understand God's love, which He sacrificially demonstrated in the death of Christ, you will be satisfied and peaceful. Your heart will be at rest from worries, passions, and unhealthy aspirations in life. What relationship can be more than that with the greatest, wisest, most powerful, and most wealthy Person in the universe? What achievement can be greater than a love relationship that gives you the best self-satisfaction in life, which is what being in relationship with God gives a Christian. You may have watched some "Christians" complain about life, make their lives better through corruption, or live in unreserved immorality. Let that not be discouraging because there are many who call themselves Christians, but who are not. Satan also has his agents in the church. Do not watch Christianity. Instead, as David said, **"Taste and see that the Lord is good; blessed is the one who takes refuge in him" (Psalm 34:8, NIV).** How do you get into that love relationship?

Accept that God loves you and has a wonderful plan for you.

Sin separated you from God such that you are not enjoying His love and plan for you.

Jesus died to take away your sins.

---

[3]Henry_Blackaby,bereanbiblechurchfm.com_unit_3:_god_pursues_a_love_relat ionship_highlights_and_scripture_notes

Confess your sins and ask Him to come into your heart and make you a new person. Then, trust Him and walk daily according to His Word. Certainly, you will look back at all that you had as successes in life and be able to say like Paul, **"But whatever were gains to me I now consider loss for the sake of Christ" (Philippians 3:7, NIV).** If you have Christ as your personal friend, you will be truly blessed and be a blessing to others. The taste of the pudding, my friend, is in the eating. Jesus is ready for you with opened arms to give you rest. Accept His invitation into this great friendship, and you will have the best in life, in Jesus' Name.

THE LORD IS YOUR PROTECTION!

In the world of advanced technology, advanced knowledge and great civilization, fear is still a great factor in the hearts of most people. This is because this "civilized" world is also a world of great selfishness, jealousy, show of power, and a great lack of love. The fact that the world is coming together so much does not seem to convince people that caring for one another is a win-win needed action. It is so hard to trust anyone in such an environment, yet so difficult to live or feel free without some level of trust.

It is sometimes hard to understand the world and its people! In my country, elections in the senate returned the nation into a one-party system, with one political party winning all electable seats in the senate. In this century? Is this a return to what someone calls "democratic dictatorship?" In Nigeria, presidential elections produced more talks about court cases than confidence in the elected president whose age has produced endless discomforting commentaries. In America, Donald Trump regained popularity and bounced back to the White House, in spite of the court cases against him. The T-Shirt for one of his past rallies frightens some non-Americans like us. On it was written, "God, Guns, Trump." In a nation where so many innocent souls have died in the hands of disgruntled gun owners, guns are still such a factor in a presidential race! Life can be frightening if our security was only in the hands of people.

The good thing is, in the midst of frightening situations around you as an individual, around the village, city, or nation, God has a final word. Security is in His hand. Whatever frightening situation you live in, take it and take courage from David's situation. He alone faced the state of Israel under Saul. His life was so much at risk, but the hand of God was upon him. The king sought to kill him, but David had a rare combination of skill and peace. With skill he fled from place to place, doing his best to keep safe. As he did so, his heart was at peace because he knew where his protection came from. He confesses,

"The Lord is my rock, my fortress and my deliverer; my God is my rock, in whom I take refuge, my shield and the horn of my salvation. He is my stronghold, my refuge and my savior - from violent people you save me. 'I called to the Lord, who is worthy of praise, and have been saved from my enemies. The waves of death swirled about me; the torrents of destruction overwhelmed me. The cords of the grave coiled around me; the snares of death confronted me'" (2 Samuel 22:2-6, NIV).

The text tells of someone who faced death from many enemies in the most palpable way but was kept safe and then, delivered.

Beloved, David's God is your God if you indeed believe in Jesus as your Savior and Lord. The protection and deliverance David had is also available for you. Whatever your fears are; whatever or whoever it is that frightens you, and no matter how much danger is facing you eye to eye, look to God for your peace, your sustenance, and eventually your deliverance. The Lord will do it for you, and it shall be totally well with you, in Jesus' Name.

WHAT SOLUTIONS WITHOUT GOD?

Have you ever been in a situation where you work hard for something and after spending so much time it boils down to nothing? I still feel the pain of work we did at a sister's wedding long ago. We had worked tirelessly to set up the hall for the reception. In the morning of the wedding day, all was well. We happily left for the church but by the time we came back the hall was completely rearranged and everything unrecognizable to us. The frustration was high. Sometimes I feel like that is what the world is like; struggling to make things work without the Creator of the universe and the Sustainer of all humanity.

Putin accused the West for the war in Ukraine and the West called the war, "Putin's War." This reminds me that there was a time in the late 1990s when there was great celebration of the end of the Cold War. Friendly diplomacy paved the way for peace, and it sounded like the world was at its best in international relations. In this century, war raged on in Ukraine, dividing the western bloc of nations and the eastern bloc made up principally of Russia, China, North Korea and Iraq. What happened to the Post-Cold War diplomacy that brought down the Berlin Wall? What happened that the permanent members of the United Nations could not stop the war, UN Resolutions fell on deaf ears, and thousands died and are still dying? Could it be that the best of these human thoughts has not given God a chance to speak to these nations and help them relate well?

Israel had absolute confidence because they faced a small nation called Ai. Joshua did the right thing militarily by spying on the land. The recommendation from his military intelligence was followed very well,

"When they returned to Joshua, they said, 'Not all the army will have to go up against Ai. Send two or three thousand men to take it and do not weary the whole army, for only a few people live there.' So, about three thousand went up; but they were routed by the men of Ai, who killed about thirty-six of them. They chased the Israelites from the city gate as far as the stone quarries and struck them down on the slopes. At this the hearts of the people melted in fear and became like water" (Joshua 7:3-5, NIV).

What an embarrassment! Joshua went to God and realized they had tried doing things without God. Well, he made things right and:

"Then the Lord said to Joshua, "Do not be afraid; do not be discouraged. Take the whole army with you and go up and attack Ai. For I have delivered into your hands the king of Ai, his people, his city and his land" (Joshua 8:1, NIV).

Joshua did just that and got things totally under control.

Beloved in the Lord, remember that God is looking and listening to you, and desiring to guide you into the way that leads to a meaningful and satisfying life. Do not walk in your own wisdom. Let God guide you in small and great things. Do not take things for granted but commit all to His grace and guidance. Pray that this world may know that all human wisdom put together without God can only lead us to some extent, but God has lasting solutions to the problems of the world He created and sustains. Move as God leads and it shall be well with you and yours, in Jesus' Name.

When we talk about healing, the first thing that comes to mind is physical sickness. But God heals from all kinds of pain. And, yes, we live in a world of pain. The war in Ukraine sent shockwaves across the globe, affecting every aspect of life, making life more difficult. This reminds me of the early 1990s in my part of the world when, because of the Structural Adjustment Plan, the government reduced salaries while there was a general rise in prices. It was a tough time. Yet, that was when most civil servants realized that they needed to invest both in individual houses and in businesses. Amid the economic crisis, God healed many from a consumption-dominated mindset. That has changed the look of most urban cities in my country. And now?

There were stories of at least a country that moved from importing very scarce wheat from Ukraine, to producing enough to feed their nation and even export some. That ability had been there but was shielded by their ability to import. While they cried about the war, they celebrated their development. Healing from a dependent mindset is critical healing needed for spiritual, physical and emotional health.

Dearly Beloved, if you need healing from illness, pray. God heals and He does so through the simple prayer of a believing individual like you. If you are traumatized, stretch out your hand to God because Jesus is the Prince of Peace and joy is a gift of the Holy Spirit. If your community is being oppressed, cry out to God and work for its liberation. You need healing! If your nation is paralyzed in growth, remember God's promise:

"If my people, who are called by my name, will humble themselves and pray and seek my face and turn from their wicked ways, then I will hear from heaven, and I will forgive their sin and will heal their land" (2 Chronicles 7:14, NIV).

The background of this text is God's warning that should the nation turn from Him to worship other gods, He would shut up rain from the heavens and send plagues on the land and locusts to eat up their plants. While God can still shut up rain from the heavens or release much heat for global warming, He can also do what He did for Israel: send a lying spirit to create confusion for a stubborn king. When the nation is ruled by lies and deception, the people suffer. The greatest lies devastating Africa in particular as well as other parts of the world are the more you get for yourself, the better. So, some businessmen and women exploit and enslave buyers with excessive and inflated prices for super-high profit margins. Some politicians and civil servants funnel public funds into personal bank accounts and use a little of it to bribe the people, so they remain poor managers. Some pastors have turned their churches into personal business enterprises. In such a world, please join me and pray for healing from a personal gain mentality. Let's pray that God's instructions to Israel in Babylon would be understood by all who work for public good: **"Seek the peace and prosperity of the city.... Pray to the Lord for it, because if it prospers, you too will prosper" (Jeremiah 29:7, NIV).**

Child of God, it is in the prosperity of your family that your own prosperity can give you peace. It is in the prosperity of your village or community that you can have opportunities to prosper. It is in the prosperity of your nation that you and your descendants can have opportunities to grow and stay safe. Look out of yourself and help others do the same, then, we would bear each other's burdens and become better and be healed from all sorts of pain by God's grace. May that be our portion, in Jesus' Name.

NOT TOO FAR BUT GETTING TOO LATE!

God is patient with us, but His patience does run out. When it does, it is dangerous. The world has become too sinful and there is a yearning for change. Can we have another revival as has occurred many times in the past in Europe and America? On February 8, 2023, a group of one hundred students started a worship service at Asbury University, Kentucky, USA. The service did not stop at the normal time. Instead, it continued for many days. On February 14 over three thousand people attended the service. Just over ten days after it started, the seminary president closed the service in order to balance worship and the academic needs of the students. He noted that the service was revealed in a deep spiritual hunger.

We live in an era of spiritual hunger indeed. In the West, many people are beginning to realize that life is not about having everything we need materially. The rich are as brokenhearted as the poor. There are even more divorces among the rich than among the poor. The educated lead society in directions with which they themselves are not too comfortable. Everyone complains and looks on helplessly, as the world drifts into a meaningless life of occultism, drunkenness, immorality, and violence seriously promoted by the movie industry and the media. Yes! We need a revival from the pulpit to the pew, from the presidency to the ghettos. We need it!

Beloved, a revival is a time of genuine return to the Lord in passionate, true spirituality. When the world and its people become so far away from God, the Holy Spirit moves more seriously, touching hearts and bringing them to God in Christ, through the reading and preaching of His word. Past revival experiences were great movements that had national and international impact. But, dear friend, national or international revival is not as important *to you* as a personal revival. No matter how national a revival experience is, there will still be unsaved people, though it will impact every aspect of national life including politics and the economy. When you have a personal revival, you are drawn closer to Jesus and, even if your economic or social situation does not change, you are better placed to cope with it joyfully, while trusting God for change. Are you passionate for Christ or do you need a revival?

If you want peace and prosperity, beloved in the Lord, this verse is for you:

"Submit to God and be at peace with him; in this way prosperity will come to you. Accept instruction from his mouth and lay up his words in your heart. If you return to the Almighty, you will be restored: If you remove wickedness far from your tent [heart]" (Job 22:21-23, NIV).

It is a personal decision you make. The tricky part of this is that you never sin too much for God to forgive and restore you to Himself, yet the more you remain in sin and not repent, the further you drift away from God's peace, prosperity, and His Kingdom. Worst of all, you cannot say when your day of death will arrive. That is why the Bible says, **"Today, if you hear his voice, do not harden your**

hearts" (Hebrews 3:7b-8a, NIV). The emphasis is on *today, now.* It can start with you and spread to the nation and beyond. It can start with you and end with you, but it would have changed your life for its best. You have given yourself to sin. It has taken away your peace and the peace of your family. You are drifting too far! Death could surprise you! Turn back before it is too late. For your joy and prosperity, return to God for His will is good, pleasing, and perfect and will make your life its very best, and you a great blessing to many, in Jesus' Name.

INJUSTICE!

We were having a conversation about the state of our nation when my friend reported his friend had said if the nation's present state of affairs and government were to change for things to be good, he would be the first to leave the country. I was baffled! "Why would someone leave the country if it gets better?" I asked. My mouth gaped opened and remained so for a while, when he explained: "Cameroon is the only country where you can move from extreme lack to extreme riches in a matter of a few months, through corruption." He may be exaggerating, but when you see some investments and people's houses around the nation and think of what they do for a profession, you cannot but say, injustice pays!

Communities have fought when they should not. Individuals have had horrible relationships when they should not. People have died and others ran out of their communities and nation when they should not. Why? Injustice does not only prevail in many nations but has even become a law in some. It is as if the best use of any level of authority for most people is to make money out of it. Even some wives make use of their authority in the kitchen to own very expensive handbags, and their husbands think food is more expensive than before! God cannot smile on either such a nation and such people, or both, who abuse justice for wealth. In a country where a journalist said, "Justice is bought and sold at the price of the highest bidder," it is important to know that God says:

"Woe to him who builds his palace by unrighteousness, his upper rooms by injustice, making his own people work for nothing, not paying them for their labor. 'But your eyes and your heart are set only on dishonest gain, on shedding innocent blood and on oppression and extortion'" (Jeremiah 22:13, 17, NIV).

Beloved, practice justice at your level of living for several reasons:

• The unjust shall not go free and it does not end well for them. God once said of a corrupt people: **"He will have the burial of a donkey - dragged away and thrown outside the gates of Jerusalem" (Jeremiah 22:19, NIV).** If you doubt this end of the unjust, read modern African and world history!

• Hunger will not kill you. God will provide for you. God reminded the unjust Israel,

"Did not your father have food and drink? He did what was right and just, so all went well with him. He defended the cause of the poor and needy, and so all went well. Is that not what it means to know me?" declares the Lord" (Jeremiah 22:15b-16, NIV).

When you do what is right and just, it goes well with you because God cares and provides for you. He will take care of you and it shall be well. God will provide for you by His grace and His abundance. Trust Him!

• Your nation will suffer injustice. God did not spare Israel. God said it for Israel, and it will be said of corrupt nations:

"The sin of the people of Israel and Judah is exceedingly great; the land is full of bloodshed and the city is full of injustice. They say, 'The Lord has forsaken the land; the Lord does not see'" (Ezekiel 9:9, NIV).

The Lord does not seem to see when injustice is overwhelming, *especially among a people who call on His name!*

• God is just. He will judge justly at the end of your life. **"Your throne, O God, will last for ever and ever; a scepter of justice will be the scepter of your kingdom" (Psalm 45:6, NIV).** He rules in justice. If Adam and Eve had taken God seriously, humanity would not be in this mess of sin and lawlessness where we are today. Please do not be like Adam and Eve and think that the story of hell is meant to frighten people. No! Those with sins of injustice and other sins, head for destructive pain and agony for eternity in hell. Dear friend, you can escape it. No matter how bad and corrupt you are, no matter how much you have soiled your hands in injustice, Jesus can cleanse you and give you life for this earth and for eternity. Flee injustice! Flee unrighteousness, give your heart to Jesus and you will live in eternity and make your nation good for you and your descendants, in Jesus' Name.

WATCH OUT FOR WICKEDNESS HIDDEN IN LOVE!

I love fishing, but I did not do the industrial type. No! We moved along the streams and rivers with hooks, on which we hung bait, threw it into the water, and caught whatever fish tried to eat the bait. Sometimes the bait used did not cost us anything. For example, we would get to the riverside, get millipedes from the mud and use them. Many times we went home with enough fish for dinner for a few days. I can imagine when a fish sees bait it does not think of it as a deceptive device but as food, not knowing it is "poisoned food!"

God has given animals to humanity as food. But when this same operation is applied from humanity to humanity, God calls it wickedness and tells us, **"There is no peace," says the Lord, "for the wicked"** (Isaiah 48:22, NIV). There are many faces of wickedness, the worst of which is the one dressed in language and a hypocritical display of love.

The greatest wicked love has been in the practice of colonialism and neo-colonialism. At the time when the world was discussing paid compensation, the French president was talking about a committee to study the history of a French presence in Cameroon and Africa! Does that mean he does not know how his country exploits Africa? When he visits without a clear, announced motive, only ignorant people take it as a visit of love. The fallout of the visit can only be to enrich his country, not the "fish" into whose pond he came.

Yes, I have also heard Cameroon, talking about writing the nation's history; this at a time when clear history demanded a political discussion for peace to return to the restive part of the country. The people's cry against marginalization sounded like fish crying out to a fisherman who does not understand the voice or language of the fish. That too is wickedness!

The worst wickedness I have seen is in a small community that sat at talks and got up to disregard all decisions taken there. It exploited both the hearts of money-minded administrators and the weakness or smallness of the other community to inflict pain and take away with pure impunity what did not belong to them. They shout out the old adage, "Might is right!" Really? When humanity rejoices in wickedness, Satan laughs because his day of destruction is coming!

Before you smile at these examples and see your inculpability, look at your own life! Do you tell your wife or husband and children you love them, but do not care about their wellbeing? Have you been smiling at someone coming to your office over and over, telling them the file they seek is missing while you keep it in a locked drawer? Is there a woman or man suffering because you "loved" them, exploited that individual and dumped him or her for a richer person?

Dear friend, God sees the small, big and biggest acts of wickedness. Disguising it in love does not change it or blind God to it. Do not be deceived. If you remain in wickedness, you will cry like the Israelites, **"We hoped for peace but no good has come, for a**

time of healing but there is only terror" (Jeremiah 8:15, NIV).
Only in repenting, in seeking the good of others, in loving with and
like Jesus, and only in genuinely saying "I am sorry," can the wicked
gain peace and enjoy life again. Ah! God, deliver us from "wicked
love," free us from wickedness in impunity and free us of all acts
of wickedness, in Jesus' Name.

FREEDOM IS EXPENSIVE!

Someone in my community moves around with a frightening, funny-looking, yet authoritative cap on his head. He told me it is what his father wore when he was fighting in the First World War. He is very proud and confident when he wears it and tells me it attracts much attention to himself. For his father, it was worn as protection from the bullets of the enemy. For the son, freedom's price has already been paid, so the cap is his toy, a thing for people to admire. Freedom looks free but it is expensive.

God is very conscious that freedom is expensive. After all, the freedom we have in Christ looks free, but it cost His life. This remembrance should be kept deep in the heart:

"Do you not know that your bodies are temples of the Holy Spirit, who is in you, whom you have received from God? You are not your own; you were bought at a price. Therefore honor God with your bodies" (1 Corinthians 6:19-20, NIV).

Paul's rhetorical question does not call for an answer but calls for reaction. If your freedom was bought:

- Honor Him who bought it. The West that has lived through many wars, has a Remembrance Day dedicated in memory of the soldiers who fought and still fight to give them freedom. If earthly freedom, here today and lost tomorrow, is that honored, what honor should be given to the One who gave you freedom that lasts until eternity?

- The Bible is clear that freedom should not be used as a license to sin. We do not have freedom so we can live any way we choose; we have freedom so we can celebrate and worship the God who gave it to us.
- Remember those who are not enjoying the freedom you have! Many are being tormented by the devil. They need freedom and you can help them enjoy what was bought for them at a price they cannot pay, Jesus' sacrificial death on the cross.

Beloved in the Lord, remember and pray for those who are struggling for freedom in the world; political freedom from colonial rule, economic freedom and freedom to live a simple self-sponsored life without the oppressive hand that checks every step one takes. Promote them. Help them. It is your Christian duty! **"Learn to do right; seek justice. Defend the oppressed. Take up the cause of the fatherless; plead the case of the widow" (Isaiah 1:17, NIV)** and you will be pointing the way to Jesus for someone's freedom. There is no greater blessing you can give one than the blessing to be free. You are blessed to be free. Therefore, also bless someone with freedom and God will be glorified, in Jesus' Name.

THINK OF THE END!

One of the strangest things life holds is that people do things without thinking of where their actions may lead them. Many, especially the wicked, are surprised by their very end. One was so arrogant and boastful in his wickedness that it was easy to conclude that he was a wizard. He stole from the family with impunity, abused whoever he wanted, challenged the security of the family, and boasted of his invincibility in the community. At last, his acts and the guilt and unpopularity he gathered sent him out of the village in self-exile. Sadly, when his end came, he did not even have the opportunity to confess or repent. He suffered acute discomfort and was silenced until he died! The other was a man who made us laugh in class in our primary school days by putting some seeds on the teacher's chair that made the teacher develop serious itching all over his body once he sat on them. We laughed as children, but the scene was very nasty; so was the boy's death some years after he was dismissed from class. Wickedness pays badly!

Sadly, history is not a great teacher to many. From Adolf Hitler to Idi Amin (who ate human flesh) and from Saddam Hussein to Bin Laden, the message of the wicked end of wickedness, even in the highest office of the land, should be heard clearly by many. Yet wickedness thrives! Solomon saw it all and told us: **"The righteous hate what is false, but the wicked make themselves a stench and bring shame on themselves. Righteousness guards the person of integrity, but wickedness overthrows the sinner"**

(Proverbs 13:5-6, NIV). The wicked make themselves a stench! When the righteous pass by, the crowds struggle to see and appreciate them. When the wicked pass by, the crowds turn away because they are a stench, an unworthy sight! Their sins overthrow them at the end. The problem is many others often suffer the effect of their wickedness as they kill before they die!

Beloved in The Lord:

- Is your community or nation suffering the effect of wicked leadership or some wicked people? Ask God for mercy and pray that He may shorten the time of your suffering.

- Pray for their repentance. No matter how wicked they may be, remember that God is not excited by the death of the wicked because hell is their final destination. God does not want anyone to perish.

- Ask the Spirit to lead you to talk to the wicked person around you and call him or her to repentance.

- Check your heart. Cleanse it from all forms of wickedness and impurity; both the least and greatest. Avoid the wrath of God!

Dear friend, while the wicked perish in shame, the righteous and godly thrive and bring joy to others. "The righteous hate what is false." Beloved, have a deep hatred for falsehood. The righteous are guarded by integrity. Let integrity be your mark, your passion and your purpose. God will be glorified, and you will be blessed and bless those around you, in Jesus' Name.

DO NOT BE A "JEALOUS" RAINDROP!

We trekked long distances sometimes to or from our rice farms. In the rainy season, we had to study the weather before setting out. Especially when it rained heavily, it was hard to cross the river that easily flooded and became very dangerous. With all our knowledge of the weather, there were times when it looked beautiful and we would leave to go, just to be embarrassed by heavy rain. Our description of such rain was "jealous rain" because it came to destroy 'enjoying brethren' like a jealous attacker.

Life has jealous attackers of enjoying brethren. These are people who come in to cause people pain and suffering when life is going well.

- Your life is going well in the office until a new worker comes in, feels you are getting what he should get, mounts attacks and will stop at nothing until he replaces you!

- Your family is doing well; then one member goes to look for wealth and is told that it must cost him or her somebody's life. The rest of the family become bait for his wealth-fishing hook.

- The village is doing well, then a gang of witches and wizards conspire to be "invisibly rich" in human flesh and bring forth much sickness, early death, or much suffering of various sorts in the village. They are jealous raindrops.

- A nation is doing well, then a wicked, ignorant and selfish leader takes over. I have seen leadership at local levels as a dangerous bomb with a combination of ignorance and wickedness. Such leaders perpetuate bribery, corruption, and killing. They ignore the suffering and death of their subjects and fix their eyes on their wealth and health, deciding to consciously forget that someday their lives will end with all they gather. Human "raindrops" are great interrupters of peaceful, joyous, and prosperous opportunities, but their hands are short.

God's statement to such raindrops is simple but firm:

"…They are like unreasoning animals, creatures of instinct, born only to be caught and destroyed, and like animals they too will perish. They will be paid back with harm for the harm they have done. These people are springs without water and mists driven by a storm. Blackest darkness is reserved for them" (2 Peter 2:12a-13, 17, NIV).

And for the wicked rain drops *in the church*,

"If they have escaped the corruption of the world by knowing our Lord and Savior Jesus Christ and are again entangled in it and are overcome, they are worse off at the end than they were at the beginning. It would have been better for them not to have known the way of righteousness than to have known it and then to turn their backs on the sacred command that was passed on to them" (2 Peter 2:20-21, NIV).

Wickedness and a destructive heart have no place in the blessings of God. God will punish evil here on earth and hereafter. Do not be a "jealous" human raindrop! The way out is life in Christ and love for your people. Let Christ cleanse your heart of all wickedness, give you peace and make you a shower of blessing, in Jesus' Name.

WHEREVER YOU ARE, GOD'S LOVE IS THERE

In our world of acute imbalance, some parts are known as developed first-world countries while others are known as underdeveloped third-world countries. The developed parts of the world are neither older civilizations nor older in the age of their existence on earth. When you see in the farming communities in America, for example, that the farm of one person is larger than the farms of all the farmers of my two villages of Ntumbaw and Njirong (Cameroon) put together, you can be tempted to ask God why. That America is well developed, and Cameroon is not, makes it easy for America to be seen as a safe haven; a place where even lazy people survive comfortably. But why are Cameroon, Niger, Kazakhstan, among others not safe havens? Did God cheat others in the distribution of land? Did God put all the intelligent people in some parts of the world and not in others? No!

The Incarnate Christ came to bring salvation to a broken world. It was scattered at Babel and is now well advanced in racism, tribalism and all forms of selfish pursuit. The best, most friendly diplomacy of the giant nations still fights for their interests first, then shares the crumbs with the unequaled nations. Jesus brought love to all nations. He started from Israel, changed the hearts of a few people and filled them with the grace to bear burdens and reach out with His love, expressed in the gospel. Jesus told the disciples to wait for the Holy Spirit and be empowered. **"But you will receive power when the Holy Spirit comes on you; and you will be my** witnesses in Jerusalem, and in all Judea and Samaria, and to the ends of the earth" (Acts 1:8, NIV). Being Christ's witnesses means spreading the experiential love of God to the world He loved. He gave His Son to die for all people in the entire world. Such love!

Wherever you are and wherever you go, know that God's love is there. He desires that everyone should come to salvation and enjoy His grace. You will not find God in any part of the world more than in others. God will not come to your world better or more than He is already there. Rather your people need to come to Him more seriously than they do now. Wherever you are, God has placed you there. Why?

"... so that they [you] would seek him and perhaps reach out for him and find him, though he is not far from any one of us. 'For in him we live and move and have our being.' As some of your own poets have said, 'We are his offspring'" (Acts 17:27-28, NIV).

Beloved, in God you move. Christ makes the world's situation better. Where things are not at their best, Christ, not religion is needed. You will be blessed if you are a channel of God's love where you are, and you will bless many by making Christ's love felt among them. Let's make the world a better place with Christ's love, in Jesus' Name.

GOD IN THE CITY

When my grandfather entered the waters of River Mantumbaw for Baptism, unbelievers standing by and watching were more upset than anyone else. While the church was singing and praising God for the transformation and the new era for the village, the rest wondered why a traditional ruler would remove his cap (traditional taboo) and get baptized. That was the dawn of a new era for the village; one in which the leader asked God for wisdom in village matters.

While we desire peace in the public place as well as peace in our hearts, we think of Christianity as a source of peace in the heart, but not as a source for social peace. Often, we see peace as a result of good governance, good development programs and a good education system. Does God see peace this way?

"As he [Jesus] approached Jerusalem and saw the city, he wept over it and said, 'If you, even you, had only known on this day what would bring you peace - but now it is hidden from your eyes. The days will come upon you when your enemies will build an embankment against you and encircle you and hem you in on every side. They will dash you to the ground, you and the children within your walls. They will not leave one stone on another, because you did not recognize the time of God's coming to you'" (Luke 19:41-44, NIV).

Such trouble awaited Jerusalem because they did not recognize the time of the Lord's coming to them. The world from village to nations and at large still fails to recognize God in the city. Looking for peace without God is an exercise in futility.

How does God come into the society, the community, and the city? Certainly, Jesus is not going to ride into any community on a donkey, horse or in the best of cars. God comes to the city in two ways:

First, by the salvation of souls. As long as the majority of the community remains unbelieving of Jesus, the Prince of Peace, the coming of peace in the community remains farfetched. The best human righteousness is filthy rags to God because neither intelligence nor political maturity produces character or righteousness. People need the Prince of Peace in their hearts. Then, His light can shine from within and produce results.

Second, God is brought into the community by having institutional leadership in the wisdom and power of God. When the village fon (leader), city mayor, governor, or head of state listens to God and obeys, he or she brings God into the community. However, the more there are active Christians in the institutions of the community including school boards, business management, hospital boards, parliament or senate and city council among others, the more Christ will be visible, and the more peace would be made to reign in the community through that institution.

One of the greatest errors Christians make is to pray more and act less, stay more with Christ and less with the community, and talk more in church but be almost totally silent in the community. They then spend all their energy rebuking demons of war, poverty, poor governance, and demons responsible for a bad economy. Jesus' approach and call on His disciples as Christians is different. He says,

"You are the light of the world. A town built on a hill cannot be hidden. Neither do people light a lamp and put it under a bowl. Instead they put it on its stand, and it gives light to everyone in the house. In the same way, let your light shine before others, that they may see your good deeds and glorify your Father in heaven" (Matthew 5:14-16, NIV).

Beloved in Christ, your Christianity lived in church and at home is a "lamp under a bowl." Your community is your church's "hill" and the "church as a city." You as a Christian must shine on that hill for the community to receive light. Your community, your workplace, and your market are your table as an individual. Put the light of Christ in you on that table so everyone can see and worship God. Then, we can have social peace. May the Holy Spirit abiding in you use your life to bring God into your community and to open the eyes of the people to see Him, accept Him and be at peace individually and socially, in Jesus' Name.

GOD ON THE THRONE

A group of friends and I were discussing the scripture and one quoted **Proverbs 29:2, (NIV): "When the righteous thrive, the people rejoice; when the wicked rule, the people groan."** I was shocked with the comment from one of us when he asked, "And when did the righteous ever rule?" That embarrassed me because I know that I have seen Christians in leadership positions. I was happy that the discussion did not follow that question because if it did, one would have asked what changed, if anything at all, when those "righteous ones ruled." If pastors and trained church leaders have problems ruling churches where the people in the pews are supposedly Christians, what do we expect of Christian leaders in non-religious institutions where they are faced with the advice and pressure of wicked, selfish people daily?

Thomas Jefferson did not help very much when he introduced the idea of Christianity and politics rather than Christian politics calling it separation of church and state. He was writing to a Baptist Association in 1802 when he said that religion was "'a matter which lies solely between Man & his God,' and that government should not have any influence over opinions," (Thomas Jefferson).[4] That sounds good at face value. But in 1779 Thomas Jefferson introduced the Virginia Statute of Religious Freedom. It became law in 1786 and separated Virginia government from any

---

[4] Thomas Jefferson, Separation of Church and State, Teachinghistory.org

established church asserting religious opinions of men were not the business of the government. Today, Christians are made to feel psychologically obliged to live dual lives while in public responsibility: Christianity at home and church, and "politics" in the office. When the wicked want to do havoc and exercise wickedness with impunity, they just tell you the church and state have nothing in common or "we are a secular state!"

Some time ago, I listened to seasoned political figures discuss. I smiled when I heard one describe the other's contributions to the rightness and integrity of the office where he worked. In his response, he explained how he made sure that the neighborhood where he lived felt his positive presence. The rest explained to him that they were finding ways and means to fix the roads in their area (where we were). He took the phone and called an official encouraging him to get the work accomplished and influence the lives of people. **"When the righteous triumph, there is great elation; but when the wicked rise to power, people go into hiding" (Proverbs 28:12, NIV).**

Dear leader, when someone on the throne is boldly and seriously rejecting the presence of Christ in leadership, examine his lifestyle. Mostly, you will see that he is looking for a license for wrongdoing. When you find yourself in any leadership position remember:

- Leadership is not salvation. God will not open heaven for you because you are a leader, no matter how many great things you do in that position. Heaven will be opened for you *only* if you have a living faith in Christ Jesus. Pay attention to your individual life.

- As a leader, at whatever level and whatever capacity, you are God's servant appointed by Him to punish those who do wrong and reward those who do right. God will judge you accordingly.

- God stands by you to enable you to succeed. He is more interested in your success than in your judgment. That is why God directs the hearts of kings. If you are in leadership, God has your heart in His hand and His heart. If you do not let Him work, you will do little, and even those who encourage you against the Lord will turn around and judge you for not yielding many results.

Let God sit on the throne of your life and use you to rule. If you are not in any leadership responsibility, pray persistently for a connection of the heart of your leader to God. When God is on the throne of men, the people are super blessed with life and peace. May you and your nation be blessed, in Jesus' Name.

THE KING'S HEART: A BATTLEGROUND!

God is particularly interested in the heart of leaders because of the influence of their decisions on lives. Yet leaders, especially in a democratic society, are expected to listen to their people and act according to their thoughts and desires.

As part of the outreach we were doing in a village, we went into the palace to share with the fon (ruler of the village). He received us quite well and listened to the message of the cross. He responded that he did not need Jesus Christ because people in authority, like him, communicate directly with God. He was not ready to yield to the scripture, **"No one who denies the Son has the Father; whoever acknowledges the Son has the Father also" (1 John 2:23, NIV).** Jesus is the Mediator between God and humanity, and no one gets to the Father but through Him. Our reading of the fon's response was that since the traditions of his people was well soaked in mysticism, he thought such mysticism was equal to communing with God. Interestingly, he created a "church" in his palace some years later. What he taught there is another matter, but clearly, his mind was an intense battleground.

God is involved in directing the heart of the leader, **"The king's heart is like a stream of water directed by the Lord; he guides it wherever he pleases" (Proverbs 21:1, NLT).** God's guidance must be accompanied by human obedience; a yielding to God for the heart to move to the direction of God's choosing. The place of freewill is a little complicated but has its place in our daily walk with

God. However, God always has the final say because He determines the course of world history and that, often through leadership decisions.

Remember how Israel got divided into two kingdoms? Rehoboam rejected the wise advice of the elders and listened to the youth, became harsh and made Jeroboam take the greater part of the nation away from Judah.

"So the king paid no attention to the people. This turn of events was the will of the Lord, for it fulfilled the Lord's message to Jeroboam, son of Nebat through the prophet Ahijah from Shiloh" (1 Kings 12:15, NLT).

Beloved leader: traditional ruler, politician, administrator, pastor, or whatever leadership responsibility you have, be focused on God. Learn to listen to Him and obey Him always. Listen to your people but take their counsel to God for confirmation or adjustment. Always have the final say, *as God speaks to you.*

Beloved in The Lord:

- •Pray for your leader always knowing that his heart is a battleground. Pray more and criticize less.
- Remember that bad leadership decisions may be God's way of directing or redirecting events and history. God hardened Pharoah's heart to liberate Israel and cause other nations to fear Him. He can do the same today.
- When leadership is bad, God could be calling the people's attention back to Himself. Instead of spending more time

criticizing leadership, spend time seeking God, making things right with Him, and praying for a revival. Remember, a good leader among wicked people cannot do much.

- Be ready to lead! Christian, be ready to lead when you hear God's voice. The greatest requirement for effective leadership is the ability to hear and obey God. When the righteous (those made right by faith in Christ Jesus) rule, the city rejoices. Why? They lead people in the counsel of the Lord which is always right. Lead at whatever level and in whatever institution God gives you as an opportunity.

Blessed is the leader whose heart is with God and blessed are the people whose leader is in tune with God in all he does. Lead with God and pray for those in leadership to lead with God and we shall all be blessed, in Jesus' Name.

HONOR YOUR NATION!

I felt I was expressing a strong commitment and joy for country when I told a friend how we used to trek over thirteen kilometers to go celebrate national youth day. To my amazement, he told me how they trekked over forty miles in his elementary school days to welcome a government official from the headquarters. That trek had been tiring but exciting. I asked if he would do the same today if he had the opportunity. "No!" He said and went on to explain that the country has changed quite negatively, and he has lost the respect and honor he had for it. Yet, he is looking forward to getting his family back home sooner or later. I was touched by the fact that having a family home is not enough to honor the nation.

Somehow, God, who created all of us and determined the exact place where we should each live, has certainly put some connectedness in our hearts about "home." God made it clear to Israel that they would be away from a home for seventy years, yet, when they got to Babylon they never felt like they were where they should even invest. God had to give them a strong message,

"This is what the Lord Almighty, the God of Israel, says to all those I carried into exile from Jerusalem to Babylon: 'Build houses and settle down; plant gardens and eat what they produce. Marry and have sons and daughters; find wives for your sons and give your daughters in marriage, so that they too may have sons and daughters. Increase in number there; do not decrease. Also, seek the peace and prosperity of the

city to which I have carried you into exile. Pray to the Lord for it, because if it prospers, you too will prosper'" (Jeremiah 29:4-7, NIV).

It was hard for them! Home is home! The reality was that it was sin that took them out of their homeland. It was sin that made it hard for them to honor homeland.

Do you realize, friend, that it is the same thing today? Globalization has not stopped people's commitment and honor for their homeland. I know many missionaries who left Europe to serve in my nation, Cameroon. None of them retired there, even when they loved the place. We hear people who cannot trace their exact family roots talking about going back home. There is a love for homeland that God has put in our hearts.

If you have a hard time honoring your nation, it must be that corruption, bad leadership, and other forms of sin that affect the socio-economic and political life of the nation are in place. Honor the nation in your heart and 1) Pray for the nation, and 2) Repent of any of the sins that contribute to people leaving the nation. When God hears your prayers and "comes to town," then, things shall change. He told Israel that when He would set up His kingdom reign on earth,

"They [Israel and us] will build houses and dwell in them; they will plant vineyards and eat their fruit. No longer will they build houses and others live in them, or plant and others eat.

For as the days of a tree, so will be the days of my people; my chosen ones will long enjoy the work of their hands" (Isaiah 65:21-22, NIV).

May The Lord implant honor for your nation in your heart and make you His agent for accomplishing such a loving, prosperous and peaceful nation that you may love and honor it more, in Jesus' Name.

YOUR LIFTING IS COMING!

Every child grows with some desire or ambition in heart. Whether those aspirations come to pass depends on many factors including how hard the child works and the nature of the environment in which the child grows. A big factor in the fulfillment of the child's future is God and His plan for that child.

Paul must have felt that he was a very successful man already. He was a great teacher of the law, bearing the name Saul. When the first wave of killings started in the first century against the church, he was there. When Stephen was being stoned to death, **"The official witnesses took off their coats and laid them at the feet of a young man named Saul" (Acts 7:58, NLT).** He was one of the most active persecutors of the church after this incident, as he would testify later. The environment in which Saul grew and worked made it look impossible for anyone to think that Saul could become a great missionary of the church. But then, who can stop God from doing what He desires to do for the one He created? God has often taken people from the rubbles of destruction, discrimination, abandonment, marginalization, oppression, and other such ills to the pinnacle of society.

I wonder what your situation is! My heart goes out to children in southern Cameroon deprived of school, teachers in Cameroon, and other civil servants who have taught and served for many years without receiving all or part of their salaries. They serve without seeing any professional advancement, sometimes for lack of money to bribe or for being nonpartisan in the country's politics. My heart goes out to people like children, students and young professionals involved in conflicts in other parts of the world fleeing places like Ukraine into an oblivious future. God has their future in His hands.

Beloved, I do not know what your situation is. I do not know the pain you are going through, and I do not know what stands in the way of your progress. I have no idea why you are concluding in your mind that there is not a bright future for you anymore. But I know one thing: as long as you believe in the Lord and depend on Him, you will be all right if you can look at your situation, hear the pessimists and conclude like the Psalmist, **"Many are saying of me, 'God will not deliver him.' But you, Lord, are a shield around me, my glory, the One who lifts my head high" (Psalm 3:2-3, NIV).**

May the Lord keep you through your troubles, make your life glorious, and lift you to heights beyond your imagination, for His glory, your blessing, and the blessing of others through you, in Jesus' Name.

WHEN VIRTUE IS LOST!

Man was created essentially good and pure. Man is born a sinner in need of salvation. Wrongdoing is easy to start, but stopping it is not that easy. Wrongdoing looks simple and enjoyable, but the consequences can be devastating and far-reaching. Wrongdoing influences a lifetime.

The other day "Luti" exclaimed in pain "Ndzeisebar" (the red dress)! We were having a celebration in the village when one night, he sneaked into a house with a girl. Unfortunately, the house owner came by. Luti was smart enough to escape but the man spotted the color of his shirt. It was red. The next day, the man searched for the boy who wore a red shirt in the night. His friends protected Luti from public shame, but it laid a block in the soil of his integrity. He is still recovering from it decades later. He knows he has been forgiven and is a committed Christian. But virtue is lost!

Noah was one of the greatest people on the earth. **"Noah was a righteous man, blameless among the people of his time, and he walked faithfully with God" (Genesis 6:9, NIV).** At this time God saw the world as wicked and decided to destroy it by flood. Noah was a virtuous man and found favor with God. He took the assignment from God, built the ark and save humanity as well as the animal and bird kingdoms. What a great man Noah was in the eyes of God and humanity. But even Noah could lose his virtue, his morality, his standard, and his excellence!

Noah's downfall happened when he planted a vine and made wine out of its fruits. The rest of the story is not so good.

"When he drank some of its wine, he became drunk and lay uncovered inside his tent. Ham, the father of Canaan, saw his father naked and told his two brothers outside. But Shem and Japheth took a garment and laid it across their shoulders; then they walked in backward and covered their father's naked body. Their faces were turned the other way so that they would not see their father naked. When Noah awoke from his wine and found out what his youngest son had done to him, he said, 'Cursed be Canaan! The lowest of slaves will he be to his brothers'" (Genesis 9:21-25, NIV).

The father's drunkenness ends in the cursing of the child! Virtue is lost! Today, there are many "Noahs" who are drunk enough with wine, are led to poverty and have sold off the future of their children for the pleasure of the cup. There are many "Noahs" who are drunk with political power and are desecrating their nation by funneling public funds into their private accounts with impunity. They do not see that they are selling off the future of their own children through exploitation, choosing who will either live in misery in their nation or live as second-class citizens in the land of their safety. Some are drunk with financial power and are spoiling them with uncontrollable open purses.

Beloved in the Lord, poverty, wealth, pride, and success or failure are all ways that can lead one to lose virtue. Even strong-will is not strong enough! Jesus does not only bring virtue, He also helps to keep it. Then, your positive impact on humanity will continue and you be sure to get a crown of righteousness in heaven. If you do not know Christ's salvation, open your heart to Him. If you are a man of great virtue, praise God, but beware! Remain committed and let His Spirit fill your heart and His word your brain. Then you will be blessed and be a blessing to others and to God's Kingdom. Jesus says: **"I tell you, he will see that they get justice, and quickly. However, when the Son of Man comes, will he find faith on the earth [in you]?" (Luke 18:8, NIV).** For your sake, for your children, for your nation and for the Kingdom, may your answer be "Yes Lord, you will find faith in me!" Keep your virtue and be blessed and be a blessing. In Jesus' Name.

PAY ATTENTION TO YOUR SINCERITY!

To be sincere is to be genuine, honest, or free from hypocrisy. There are times when your greatest peace with yourself and with God comes from your sincerity in the situation around you. I was in the first year of secondary school, young and innocent. It was my first time away from my parents, and I lived with relatives who did not have very much and who I was trekking for just over an hour, I arrived from school hungry and was met with an empty dish. There was no food to eat! There were bags of raw groundnuts by the door that the mother of the house kept for sale. I picked out two shells of groundnuts from a bag, cracked them and was eating when the daughters showed up from behind the house and saw me with the groundnuts. They were furious, reported me to their mother and for over a year my name in the house was, "Shongndzeren" (groundnut stealer)! The pain added to my hunger on that day and the struggles in the days that followed. The guilt and bad feelings were enormous. Thank God I was not close to home because I would have dropped out of school and left. My peace and joy were restored when I told myself that in reality I was not stealing, and they simply did not like me that much.

It can be hard to be a prisoner without a crime, feel bad without doing wrong, be mishandled without misbehavior, and oppressed but not a slave. In such times and situations, your greatest joy and peace come from the sincerity of your heart.

When that happens to you:

- Forgive! Remember Jesus on the cross. He was maltreated, persecuted, tortured, and crucified but He cried out to the Father, **"Father, forgive them, for they do not know what they are doing" (Luke 23:34a, NIV).** You too can forgive.

- Focus on God, not your oppressors! It is only because Jesus focused on God that He was able to talk to God favorably. If He focused on them and their misbehavior, He could have cursed them instead. Stephen also focused on God in his persecution and even had a great vision of the angels getting ready to receive his soul. He too forgave his persecutors. You too can focus on God when it is hard. The Lord will be your deliverer.

- Focus on the future! When you are sincere, know that God stands with you to accomplish things on your behalf. These things may not be obvious at the moment. Jesus' persecution for no crime ended in His death, but the blood that flew from that cross to "the earth below brought forgiveness to the world that had treated Him so."[5] Stephen's persecution and murder gave birth to the spread of the gospel.

My examples above do not mean that persecution for no wrongdoing would end in death, No! I would not have died had my name remained "Shungndzeren!" The experience did not teach me

---

[5] He Came In Love, Jimmy and Carol Owens,m.youtube.com

to steal but to be careful with my relationships with others. I made it through five years, got my certificate and left, but we remained in good relationship.

Join me in confessing sincerely like Paul:

"... as servants of God we commend ourselves in every way: in great endurance; in troubles, hardships and distresses;…in purity, understanding, patience and kindness; in the Holy Spirit and in sincere love" (2 Corinthians 6:4, 6, NIV).

May God help us to live in this manner, for in that way we will be blessed and be a blessing to others, in Jesus' Name.

THE RESURRECTED LORD IS YOUR GOD!

I went to school in the 1970s and 1980s and there was little or no fear walking around. When my friend and I went to visit other students, it happened that we were coming back home after 10:00 pm and had to pass through a raffia palm bush. It was thick and dark but also a shorter road to the house where we lived, so we took it. At one point, we heard some noise in the bush and got frightened, thinking that it was an animal or something that could harm us. We stopped for a while, looked around, and waited, armed only with some courage, had we been attacked. No thought of the possibility of it being a human being crossed our minds. When we waited for a while and never heard the noise again, we concluded that it was safe. We moved on and went home. Gone are those days in my nation. Sad!

On a few internet news pages, announcements about "missing persons" are becoming regular. Kidnapping is no longer just a thing in the war zone in the nation. We hear of it in the cities now. When one reads of what happened in the east of Cameroon, where six members of a family were killed in cold blood and the bodies mutilated and left to rot in the house, it sounds like one is in a place where insane people live. But when you read further that the mother of the house was raped, her breasts cut off and put on the table, and her kids and her sister were all killed with their bodies scattered around in the pools of their own blood, then, you know that this is not just barbarism. It is extreme wickedness. It is an indicator that Satan really lives here. To say the least, it is frightening. However, it is not surprising.

Evil cannot be surprising in a world where God and His word can be considered as too much; where teachers model corruption to their students with the help of their parents, where occultism thrives, and its promotion is no longer secret. Occults used to be known as secret societies. Today, they are venerated as sacred societies and compared to religious bodies. Sadly, this evil finds its place in the church too. There are stories of men and women of God poisoned by colleagues, and of pastors operating with powers other than God's. How could this be explained in a community of love and godliness? Sad!

Beloved of God, this is not new. Paul cried out in both despair and hope for the city of Corinth that also intertwined the good and the bad, giving room for both God and evil. And what union can there be between God's temple and idols? For we are the temple of the living God. As God said: "**I will live in them and walk among them. I will be their God, and they will be my people**" (2 Corinthians 6:16b, NIV).

- We must refuse to be comfortable when evil prevails around us. Discomfort leads to crying out to God in prayer and reaching out to bring a change.

- Christian, realize that God lives in you; the Spirit of God who resurrected Jesus from the dead lives in you. Let God use that presence to drive away fear from you, give you courage to live, and the grace to reach out and bring some change around you.

- When you meet any frightening situation, shift your eyes from the situation to God and be at peace because He is the Greatest Being in the universe who says He will be your God, and you will belong to Him. With Him, it is well with you and yours, as you keep trusting Him while praying and working for change in the rottenness around you.

Peace be upon your heart, in Jesus' Name.

Appendix

Names in "" are pseudonyms to protect the identity of people.

Many cultural and regional phrases have been retained to give cultural and regional flavor to Rev. Nfor's life in Cameroon. As he has lived throughout the world, some words and phrases reflect world-wide language diversity.

Devotions are taken from Rev. Nfor's original Pacesetter postings.

About the Author

MA of Agricultural & Political Economics, University of Aberdeen, Scotland (1991)

Worked as agro-economist, Ministry of Agriculture, Cameroon

Master of Divinity in Theology, Ogbomoso, Nigeria

Doctor of Ministry, leadership emphasis, North American Baptist Seminary, Sioux Falls, South Dakota, USA

Professor: Cameroon Baptist Theological Seminary, Ndu

Dean of International Leadership, Yaoundé University, Yaoundé, Cameroon

Pastoral Ministry: Etoug-Ebe Baptist Church (2007-2016)

Church Planting & Senior Pastor: Patmos Baptist Church, Jouvence-Mbenda, Yaoundé, Cameroon (2017-present)

Born: Ntumbaw. Rev. Nfor lives in Yaoundé, Cameroon

Notes

www.ingramcontent.com/pod-product-compliance
Lightning Source LLC
Chambersburg PA
CBHW060903280326
41934CB00007B/1169